Hamlyn all-colour paperbacks

David Burgess Wise

Veteran and Vintage Cars

illustrated by Walter Wright

Hamlyn - London
Sun Books - Melbourne

FOREWORD

What we now refer to as the golden age of the motorcar—the era prior to the 1930s, when mass production methods and "styling" became the dominant features—is arbitrarily divided into three periods: Veteran, Edwardian and Vintage.

The Veteran epoch, when self-propelled vehicles were still unreliable horseless carriages, is recognised officially as prior to January 1, 1905, but of course some vehicles built before that date were sophisticated, dependable motorcars, and some very crude machinery was marketed for several years into the next era of motoring, the "Edwardian" age (1905-18), named in honour of Britain's motorphile monarch (who died in 1911).

During this period, most of what we regard as the "modern" refinements were added to the specification of the car, and coachwork design reached unparalleled heights of elegance.

After the war comes the Vintage period (1919-30) in which some of the most magnificently engineered cars of all time were produced, power unit design took giant steps forward, and the motor car became truly established as a popular means of travel, yet still retained much of its early romance.

In writing this book, I have tried to relate cars to the period in which they operated, without being prejudiced by latter day judgments, which so often condemn cars because they fail to live up to modern standards of performance, or which laud certain vehicles because of their purely fortuitous survival.

David Burgess Wise

Published by The Hamlyn Publishing Group Limited
London · New York · Sydney · Toronto
Hamlyn House, Feltham, Middlesex, England
In association with Sun Books Pty Melbourne

Copyright © 1970 by The Hamlyn Publishing Group Limited

ISBN 0 600 00283 7

Phototypeset by Filmtype Services Limited, Scarborough
Colour separations by Schwitter Limited, Zurich
Printed in Holland by Smeets, Weert

CONTENTS

Steam Carriage Builders

Designs for horseless carriages can be found as far back as the late 15th century, but these early attempts, powered by cranks, treadles, or the wind, can have been of little use on the terrible roads of the period. Although the steam engine first appeared in the mid-17th century, it was far too clumsy for use on a carriage. From about 1680 models were made powered by aeolipyles (boilers with a narrow tube protruding from them, from which the steam issued to push the vehicle forward by reaction), but Denis Papin, who in 1690, first proposed a piston-engined car, felt that the roads would have to be improved before *"voitures par terre"* could be perfected.

Model powered by an aeolipyle, 1775

The first full-sized steam vehicle seems to have been the three-wheeled truck built by the French engineer Cugnot by order of his Government in 1769. A huge and cumbersome three-wheeler with a heavy boiler hung out ahead of the single front wheel, which was driven by twin cylinders, one either side, with their piston rods acting on ratchets on the hub, the Cugnot was intended for artillery haulage. For all its size, the boiler lacked the capacity to propel the truck at a reasonable speed, and it could only travel $\frac{5}{8}$ mile in 60 minutes.

Trevithick's 1801 carriage

A larger, more powerful version was completed in 1770, but the wavering mass of the boiler and the narrow track made it prone to fall on its side when cornering; and it was abandoned. By a freak of fate it has survived to this day, and consequently has attracted more attention than it deserves. The only remarkable feature of its design lay in the use of high-pressure steam.

James Watt, who perfected the crude steam engine of Newcomen by the invention of the condenser, had a morbid fear of high-pressure steam, and in 1784 patented a steam carriage "to keep other people from similar patents."

By "other people" he doubtless meant his assistant, William

Gurney's London-Bath coach, 1828

Hancock's private phaeton, 1838

Murdock, whose father had constructed a steam carriage in Scotland in the early 1770s, and who was passionately devoted to road locomotion, building many successful models between 1782 and 1792, when Watt's disapproval reached a head and forced him to abandon his experiments. Murdock, who pioneered the use of gas for lighting, was in charge of the assembly of Boulton & Watt engines at Redruth, in Cornwall, where they were used to pump water out of the tin workings. It was Cornwall, forcing ground of the steam engine, not Paris, which was to prove the true birthplace of the automobile.

On Christmas Eve, 1801, the villagers of Camborne, Corn-

The omnibus *Autopsy*, built by Hancock in 1833

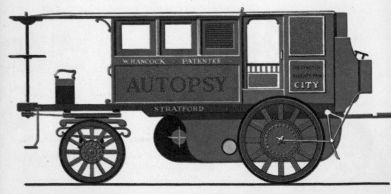

wall, saw the first successful motor vehicle in history puff steadily through the streets. With several people aboard, it climbed the 1:20 gradient of Beacon Hill "like a little bird" until it ran out of steam. The constructors were Richard Trevithick, a 30-year-old genius, the real pioneer of the high-pressure steam engine, and his cousin Andrew Vivian, who provided his financial backing. Four days later they tried another hill-climbing test, but the machine broke down, so they parked it under a lean-to and adjourned to the local hotel for "a roast goose and proper drinks." While they were feasting, the boiler ran dry, and steam carriage and lean-to went up in flames. Two years later Trevithick had another, more advanced, chassis constructed to his design by Harvey's foundry at Hayle, Cornwall, and shipped to London, where it ran successfully, but frightened the horses and received such a bad Press thereby that Trevithick dismantled it, and turned his attention to stationary engines and railway locomotives.

In 1826 another Cornishman, 33-year-old Goldsworthy Gurney, built a remarkable steam carriage, powered by steam-operated legs as well as wheels; he soon abandoned this design, and built a six-wheeled, 18-seater steam coach which enjoyed a qualified success, and in 1829 made the first long-distance automobile journey, from London to Bath. That year Gurney introduced his steam drag, a light-weight and elegant carriage which could be used in conjunction with a trailer. Limited production of these drags was undertaken, and in 1831 Sir Charles Dance used three of these vehicles on the first scheduled

Era, an 1832 Hancock 'bus

1839 Dietz *remorquer* with unique 4-2-2 wheel layout

motor bus routes in the world, between Gloucester and Chelten-
ham. Gurney, one of the most persistent of the early pioneers,
was knighted in 1863. But not for his steam carriages – it was in
recognition of the work he had done in improving the heating,
lighting and plumbing of the House of Commons.

A contemporary of Gurney was Walter Hancock, born in
1799 in Marlborough, Wiltshire. At the age of 25 he built a
steamer with an odd engine in which the pistons were replaced by rubberised bags inflated by steam. As the bags
expanded and contracted they turned a crankshaft.

Hancock soon scrapped this design in favour of a more
conventional engine. He built a twin-cylinder frontwheel-
drive tricar in which he covered hundreds of miles in the
London area. He encountered a good deal of hostility, and
decided that the best way to counter this opposition was to
start a bus service, on which the public could ride for a
reasonable fare. In 1830 he introduced *Infant*, a "toast-rack"
bodied charabanc, which started a regular service between
Stratford, then a small Essex town, and London in February
1831. Experts declared that it did not frighten horses, respond-
ed admirably to the controls, and made a favourable impression
on the passengers. Over the next few years Hancock put nine
coaches into service, pioneering regular bus services in London.

By mid-1834 Hancock had established a chain of service
stations and garages in London, and his *Era II* and *Autopsy*

("see for yourself") carried 4,000 people over the Moorgate-Paddington route at a speed of 12 m.p.h. between August and November that year. The fare was 6d, and running costs were in the region of 2d a mile. Many thousands had travelled on Hancock's coaches by the time he unveiled his crowning achievement, the 22-seat *Automaton,* in 1835. On test in the Bow Road, it carried 30 men over a measured mile at 21 m.p.h.

Experimenters like Hancock found themselves up against considerable opposition from the horse-carriage trade and the railways, and the turnpike trust, probably in the pay of both factions, charged a self-propelled carriage £2 8s and a horse-carriage only 3s to pass a tollgate. Although a Parliamentary commission in 1831 had concluded that steam carriages were practical, and the great road-builder Thomas Telford had told them "in justice steam-carriages should pay less toll than those drawn by horses," by 1840 vested interests had won the day.

However, it should be noted that in Paris, where experimenters were encouraged, progress came to a halt around the same time. The great French pioneers were Jean Christian Dietz and his two sons, Charles and Christian, whose *remorquers* of 1832-41 were road-going railway trains, pulling coaches.

'As easily managed as a child's cart' — Macerone steamer, 1835

Lenoir and Marcus

The first man to build a car powered by an internal combustion engine was the Swiss, Isaac de Rivaz, who around 1805 replaced the steam engine of a successful horseless carriage he had built with an "explosion motor" running on gas. The long vertical cylinder was open at the top, from which the piston rod protruded. Gas was admitted to the cylinder by a cock and ignited by an electric spark from a Voltaic pile. The heavy piston was pushed up the cylinder by the explosion, and when it fell, a chain rack on its rod turned a ratchet wheel linked to the front wheels by a belt. The exhaust valve was foot operated. Several times De Rivaz managed to coax the machine across a room and back, then decided it was too intractable, and built a pumping engine instead.

There was then a gap of over half-a-century before the next major step forward was taken, by Jean-Joseph Etienne Lenoir, a Belgian inventor, who around 1858 had designed a two-stroke gas engine, to market which a company was set up in the Rue de la Roquette, Paris, in 1860. By this time Lenoir had perfected his design to such an extent that it could be made small and powerful enough to drive a carriage.

Lenoir's first car was described in *Le Monde Illustré* of June 16, 1860. It was a shooting brake with a 1½-h.p. single cylinder

The 1875 Marcus Car

water-cooled engine beneath the rear seats. Ignition was electric, by Ruhmkorff coil, and transmission was direct, by chain. In 1863, Lenoir built a second car, with a $1\frac{1}{2}$-h.p. engine running on liquid hydrocarbon fuel. It was not a great success, taking three hours for a six-mile journey to Vincennes and back, but in 1864 Lenoir received an order for a motor car from Alexander II, Tsar of Russia, an ardent and progressive Francophile. The car was duly dispatched from Vincennes station – and passed into obscurity. Papers documenting the sale were unearthed in Paris in 1906, and the cellars of the Imperial Palace in St. Petersburg searched without success. Lenoir's later career was clouded by failure and poverty, for he had sold all his patent rights in 1863.

In 1864 a Viennese, Siegfried Marcus, built a crude four-wheeler running on benzene, using an engine he had designed for an airship. It was not very successful, and his other inventions engaged his attention, and only in 1875 was an improved vehicle ready for test. It was capable of 4 m.p.h., and successfully made the 16-mile round trip from Vienna to Klosterneuberg and back. He built four cars before complaints about the noise they created forced the police to prohibit them from the streets of Vienna. One of his cars is still preserved in running order in the Vienna Museum.

Lenoir's 1860 design

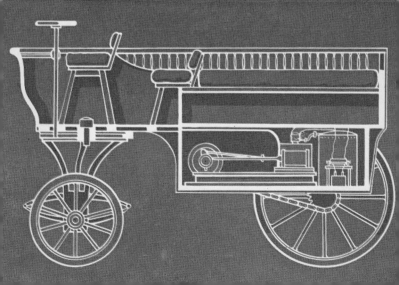

R. E. B. Crompton built *Blue Belle* in 1861, while still at Harrow

More Pioneers

The record of the early days of self-propelled traffic would not be complete without the mention of Julius Griffith, whose "steam diligence" of 1821 had gears for changing speed, and the first tubular condenser fitted to a steam carriage; most steamers right up to the beginning of the 20th century let their steam go to waste once it had passed through the engine. Built in the workshops of the celebrated engineer Joseph Bramah, the Griffith carriage lacked the boiler capacity to be a success, but its design inspired most of the steam carriage builders of the period. Noteworthy, too, was Birstall and Hill's steam coach of 1824 which had four-wheel-drive, front wheel brakes and rack and pinion steering. Alas, the weight of all these technological advances was too much for the boiler, and, after a few inconclusive tests between Edinburgh and Leith in 1826, and in London in 1827, it exploded.

Then there was Samuel Brown, who in 1826 was driving around the Woolwich area on a carriage fitted with his patent "gas and vacuum" engine, originally designed for a canal boat, which used illuminating gas as a fuel. Once, "to the satisfaction of numerous spectators," the clumsy machine (the water-

Road locomotive — the 1869 Lotz *train routier*

cooled engine was around 40 litres capacity) ascended the steep slope of Shooter's Hill. But running costs were so much greater than those of steam that the idea was dropped. It was really no more practical than Medhurst's 1800 scheme of powering vehicles by compressed air, and setting up recharging stations served by the canals, which were enjoying a boom at that time comparable to the railway boom of the 1840s.

The anti-steam-carriage legislation of 1840 onwards culminated in the 1865 Locomotive Act, which restricted steam vehicles to 4 m.p.h. on the open road, and 2 m.p.h. in towns, and compelled the carrying of a red flag by a man walking in front of the vehicle (the red flag was not compulsory after an amendment to the law in 1878, but continued in many instances to be carried for as long as the footman was required). These restrictions are usually regarded as having effectively spelled the doom of motoring in England for half-a-century; but it was only the weaker brethren who were deterred. The passenger-carrying steam coach having proved unremunerative and the light steam carriage unreliable, most British constructors turned to the traction engine, a field in which they led the world for three-quarters of a century. This was the trend in France, too, where Lotz and Larmanjat in the 1850s and 1860s were following the ideas of Dietz.

No amount of legislation could deter the keenest British enthusiasts such as R. E. B. Crompton (later a famous electrician) who began building a steam car at the age of 16 while still at Harrow School in 1861, and later pioneered passenger transport in India with three-wheeled Thomson steamers towing omnibus trailers on the Grand Trunk Road.

The main enemy of the development of the automobile in the mid-19th century was not so much hostile legislation as dilettantism; many engineers tried their hand at building self-propelled vehicles, ran them for a while, and then went on to some other project. There was no ready market for steam carriages, although Thomas Rickett went into limited production in the late 1850s with three-wheeled two-seaters, one of which was sold to the Marquis of Stafford in 1858, and another to the Earl of Caithness, who toured Scotland on it with his wife in 1860. Others who were active in England at that period were J. W. Boulton, who built half-a-dozen cars between 1848 and 1860, the Tangye brothers, who in 1868 built *Cornubia*, a three-wheeler with outside cylinders, which was exported to India, and the Yarrow & Hilditch and Garrett, Marshall & Co cars shown at the Great Exhibition in London in 1862. Most of

Yarrow & Hilditch carriage, shown at the 1862 London Exhibition

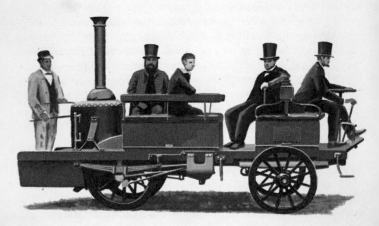

these machines lacked the elegance of the steam carriages of the 1830s, although they were undeniably more efficient. The clumsiness of appearance was mainly due to the employment of locomotive practice in their construction; the position would not change until the advent of the bicycle.

This was the great catalyst which hastened the introduction of the motorcar. Bicycle building taught engineers how to make structures which were light yet strong – wire wheels and tubular frames – and the ownership of a bicycle introduced large numbers of young men to the delights of touring without relying on the railway. It also began the reawakening of roads and hotels which had lain moribund since the railway had ousted the stage-coach. From about 1880, light three- and four-wheeled automobiles based on bicycle practice began to appear. There was the Light Steam Tricycle of Sir Thomas Parkyns, built by the Greenwich firm of A. H. Bateman & Co. shown at the 1881 Stanley Bicycle Show, and still in running order 20 years later; S. Beeney's Birmingham-built steam tricycle of 1884; the 1887 Sherrin Electric Tricycle from Ramsgate (the company was known by 1891 as Vaughan Sherrin, based in Islington and also producing Electric Bath Chairs) and the little Starley electric of 1888 constructed by the head of the Rover bicycle company. The only serious attempt at production seems to have been made by Magnus Volk, builder of the electric railway along the front at Brighton, who turned out a number of electric carriages around 1888, one of which was sold to the Sultan of Morocco, constituting the first-ever export of the British motor industry. The car was a four-wheeled dog-cart with an Immisch electric motor: three years later the Sultan ordered an ornately decorated car from the Peugeot company in France. Ten years ahead of its time was the Butler "Petrocycle" of 1887, with an internal combustion engine and spray carburetter, but it died for lack of finance, and because of the restrictive traffic laws of the time.

Incidentally, one wonders whether the story of motoring in Britain might not have been markedly different had not Prince Albert died at the age of 43 in 1861, for he had encouraged technological progress more than any other leader of society and owned an early four-wheeled velocipede.

15

Amédée Bollée

One of the most remarkable figures in what might be termed the "Dark Ages" of motoring in France was a Le Mans bell-founder, Amédée Bollée, who in 1871 set up a small workshop in his works to develop his dream, a practical horseless carriage. In 1873 he began trials of his first vehicle, a brake named *L'Obéissante*, a lofty 12-seater with all the grace of a bandstand on wheels. It featured independent suspension of the front wheels, which had Lenkensperger (Ackermann) steering. The results were so conclusive that in August 1875, the Minister of Public Works gave permission for Bollée to use *L'Obéissante* over a specified area, "provided that the driver gave three days' advance warning to the district engineer of the itinerary which would be followed".

Despite this official sanction, Bollée contrived to break 75 traffic regulations in a journey from Le Mans to Paris two months later, but a trip round Paris in the steamer caused the Prefect of Police to drop the charges.

Bollée's next vehicle was *La Mancelle* of 1878. This was almost certainly the first vehicle to have the engine in front under a bonnet, driving the rear axle by propeller shaft, bevel gears and chains, a layout that, with the addition of a gearbox, would be common to motorcars for decades to come. Moreover *La Mancelle* had independent front suspension by double transverse leaf springs.

By 1880, the automobile side of the Bollee business was employing a hundred workmen, and *Mancelles* were being turned out with either "calèche" or "postchaise" bodywork, and a "concessionaire général", M. Lecordier, had been appointed. Sales were not up to expectation, however, Lecordier was ruined, and Bollée abandoned steam carriage production, but not before producing, in 1881, *La Rapide*, a lighter vehicle seating half-a-dozen, and capable of around 40 m.p.h. His two elder sons Amédee *fils* (born 1869) and Léon (born 1870) were to make their own highly individual contributions to motoring history. Bollée *Père's* patents were acquired by Barthold, a rich Berlin banker, who had steam carriages constructed to their specifications in the Woelhert factory betwen 1880 and 1883, with which he attempted to set up public bus services in Germany, Austria, Russia and Sweden.

The scheme, far too ambitious for the period, ended with the banker's ruination.

L'Obéissante 1873

Gottleib Daimler

Gottleib Daimler was 28 when he saw his first horseless carriage in 1862. Anxious to find an alternative power unit to the steam engine, the young German had resigned from the locomotive works of F. Rollé & Schwiegne at Grafenstaden, near Strasbourg in 1861, had travelled to Paris, and then went on to England, where he acquired much experience from the leading manufacturers. The climax of his visit was a trip to the 1862 Great Exhibition, where he saw a great many traction engines, and the Yarrow & Hilditch and Garrett, Marshall steam carriages.

Back in Germany in 1863, he met a gifted young draughtsman named Wilhelm Maybach. When in 1872, Daimler was appointed manager of the Gasmotoren-Fabrik Deutz, producing Otto engines, he recommended Maybach as designer.

The Otto gas engine, like the 1805 De Rivaz unit, was a free piston machine deriving its power from the explosion of the uncompressed gas, and was noisy and pathetically inefficient. Sales fell alarmingly and to beat the crisis, Otto once more began work on a project abandoned in 1862, the four-stroke engine. The problem was ignition, for it was much more difficult to

Daimler's motorised carriage, 1885

Cannstatt-Daimler taximeter cabriolet, 1896

ignite a compressed gas; Otto evolved a slide valve arrangement (a similar device had fired Brown's 1824 "Gas-vacuum" engine) which exposed a flame to the gas at the correct moment, and the four-stroke engine became a practical reality. Although still too clumsy to drive a vehicle, it was the power source Daimler had been looking for. In 1882 he resigned from Deutz, and set up on his own in Cannstatt, where Maybach joined him as engineer and designer.

Together they worked out a simpler form of ignition, by a closed metal tube projecting from the cylinder head to the outside of the engine, and kept incandescent by a petrol burner. Using this, they were able to construct an engine which would run at the then unheard of rate of 700-900 r.p.m. In 1885, a motorcycle and a motor carriage were built. In 1890 the Daimler-Motoren-Gesellschaft was set up: between 1892-97, having quarrelled with Gottleib Daimler and Maybach, it produced rather archaic-looking horseless carriages, designed by Max Schrödter. Following a reconciliation, the Maybach-designed Phönix-Daimler range of 1897 was a major step forward. Daimler died on March 6, 1900. Maybach found it increasingly difficult to get on with the new management, and in 1907 left to join Zeppelin as engine designer.

Karl Benz

Karl Benz was born in 1848, in Karlsruhe, Germany. From an early age he showed much interest in technical subjects, and at the age of 16 he was admitted to Karlsruhe Polytechnic, where his teacher Ferdinand Redtenbacher impressed him by prophesying that a new source of power was going to supplant the steam engine.

Nevertheless, Benz's first job was with the Karlsruhe Engineering Works, locomotive manufacturers, but he left in 1866 – three years later, Gottlieb Daimler would be appointed chief engineer of the company.

In 1871 Benz set up an ''Iron Foundry and Machine Shop'' in Mannheim, but the company was soon in financial difficulty. In 1877, to alleviate his rather desperate position he began work on an internal combustion engine. It had to be a two-stroke to avoid the newly-awarded Otto four-stroke patent, and by the end of 1879, Benz' engine was running successfully. It was not until late 1883 that he was able to secure backing which would enable him to develop his designs as he wished. The demand for the Benz engines, which pioneered scavenging of the exhaust gases and coil ignition, was such that by 1886 the

Hewetson's 1895 Benz Viktoria

firm had to move to far larger premises in Mannheim. That year, Otto's patent monopoly on the four-stroke was ruled invalid as a prior registration was established (Beau de Rochas 1862), and Benz, who had begun work on a four-cycle power unit in 1884, patented a three-wheeled car with belt transmission driven by a gas engine on January 29, 1886; he tested such a car on the streets of Mannheim six months later. This was the first internal-combustion-engined car to be designed as a complete entity. By 1888, the Benz three-wheeler was in limited production: the sales literature described it as "an agreeable vehicle, as well as a mountain-climbing apparatus." However, sales were negligible, even though Benz had a Paris agent, Emil Roger, and it was not until 1893, when the four-wheeled 3-h.p. "Viktoria" model with Lenkensperger steering, but still with belt drive, was introduced, that real commercial success was achieved. A cheaper, $1\frac{1}{2}$-h.p. model, the "Vélo" was added to the range in 1894; these were the first cars in the world to be mass-produced. In 1895, 135 cars were built, including 62 Vélos and 36 Viktorias. By 1898, annual production had risen to 434, and before the end of the next year the 2,000th Benz car left the works.

1885-86 Benz three-wheeler

The 1883 Delamarre-Debouteville car

French Pioneers

Edouard Delamarre-Debouteville (born 1856) was the son of the owner of a cotton-spinning mill at Fontaine-le-Bourg, near Rouen. He had already built a successful experimental gas-engined three-wheeler, and this had inspired him in 1883 to convert an old shooting brake belonging to his brother into a motor car. This he did, with the assistance of his foreman, Malandin. He decided to use petrol instead of gas, and fitted the car with a wick-carburetter, in which petrol was vapourised by evaporation rather than by spray through a jet. A similar arrangement was used on the British Lanchester car from 1895-1915. The power unit had two cylinders; final drive was by belt.

Another remarkable Frenchman was Fernand Forest, who in 1885 built an opposed-piston engine with low-tension magneto ignition and a spray carburetter, both features more than a decade ahead of their time; in 1891 Forest, having acquired a wealthy patron, produced the world's first four-cylinder petrol engine with mechanical inlet valve operation (most early engines relied on the suction created by the piston to open the inlet valve). He concentrated on building motor-boats, built one of the earliest six-cylinder engines for the boat "Volapuk," but oddly enough does not seem to have tried his advanced power units in a motor car.

In fact, when Forest was building his engines, the French motor industry was still in the gas motor era. The Daimler stationary engines were built under licence in Paris by Panhard & Levassor, makers of wood- and metal-working machinery. In 1890 they granted the great Peugeot ironmongery firm the rights to use Daimler engines in motor carriages, and the result was so successful that in 1891 Panhard & Levassor built their first car, a rather crude horseless carriage with the engine amidships. They produced a handful of similar vehicles, and then in 1892 Levassor evolved what has perversely become known as *Le System Panhard*, in which the motor was set vertically under a bonnet at the front, driving the rear axle via a friction clutch, and a gearbox in which the various speeds were obtained by engaging gear wheels of appropriate diameters sliding on shafts. Levassor's celebrated aphorism about

The first Panhard-Levassor, 1890-91

his gearbox, based on the speed-change mechanism of a lathe, *"C'est brusque et brutal, mais ça march"* can be applied to the whole concept of the early Panhard & Levassor cars, for the gears operated in the open air without benefit of oil, the tiller steering was poorly laid out, and the massive construction of the coachwork and wheels was scarcely elegant.

By 1892 Panhard & Levassor had four different models in production, all with uncased gears and iron-shod waggon wheels (rubber tyres "which give very good results," were obtained at a 10 per cent increase in price). Coachwork was four-seated ("Dog-cart" or "Wagonnette") or two-seated. In 1893 one of these two-seaters, with Victoria coachwork, was sold to a priest, Abbé Gavois, who used it regularly for the next 40 years, hot-tube ignition and all. The 3½-h.p. V-twin engine was replaced by the new Phénix-Daimler in-line two-cylinder in 1895. Panhard & Levassor seem to have built far better Daimler engines than Daimler could, for speeds of up to 30 m.p.h. could be attained by cars fitted with the Panhard-Phénix engines, while the German-built units were incapable of propelling a vehicle at much over 20 m.p.h. In 1898 Panhard introduced wheel steering; a new four-cylinder Phénix-type engine was offered as an option in the same year. Until the

The archetypal car — 1892 Panhard

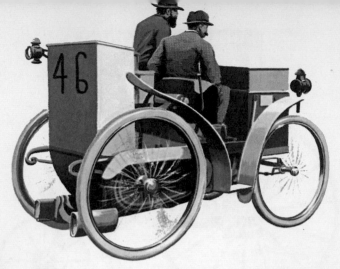

The first Michelin pneumatic tyres were tested on this 1895 Peugeot

turn of the century, Panhard cars were virtually unbeatable in competition, but the wheel turned full circle when the Cannstatt-Daimler firm introduced their new Mercedes model in 1901, and rendered the Panhard obsolescent.

Panhard's principal rivals during the 1890s were "Les Fils de Peugeot Frères," a branch of a company founded in the late 18th century. In the 1850s, Peugeot, skilled manufacturers of ironmongery, had begun making steel "whalebones" for crinolines at their Beaulieu factory, and later corset stays became a staple product. This experience in working thin metal rods stood them in good stead when they began building bicycles in the mid-1880s, under the supervision of Armand Peugeot. At the 1889 Universal Exhibition in Paris, Peugeot exhibited their first automobile, a three-wheeled steamcar built to the design of Léon Serpollet. Emil Levassor, hearing that Peugeot were not very satisfied with the performance of this vehicle, hurried to their headquarters at Valentigny to see Armand Peugeot. At that time Levassor had no interest in building cars, merely in producing and selling engines. He soon convinced Peugeot that the Daimler motor was the power unit of the future and the manufacture of light, rear-engined cars with much bicycle influence in their design began in 1890.

25

Lambert's 1891 three-wheeler

American Pioneers

The motor age in America dawned not long after Independence, for in 1787 Oliver Evans was granted a monopoly for running waggons and mills powered by steam in Maryland. The waggons remained a pipe dream until, as Evans recalled," in the year 1800, or 1801, never having found a person willing to contribute to the expense, or even to encourage me to risk it myself, it occurred to me that, although I was then in full health, I might suddenly be carried off by the yellow fever, that had so often visited our city (Pennsylvania), or by some other disease or casualty, to which all are liable; and that I had not discharged my debt of honour to the State of Maryland by producing the steam waggons; I determined, therefore, to set to work the next day to construct one." Evans' steam carriage, *Orukter Amphibolos* was a huge clumsy amphibian, designed for dredging harbours.

Around 1830, isolated pioneers, such as Harrison Dyer, of Boston, and Joseph Dixon, of Lynn, also in Massachussetts, built steamers; and Rufus Porter of Hartford, Connecticut, made a steam carriage, with the advanced feature of a differential gear, that was almost a success. However, the 1834 New York-built James carriage, which also boasted a differential, "as it was roughly built, did not long hold together." One of America's most brilliant exponents of road locomotion was J. K. Fisher of New York, who between 1840-1859 built half a dozen steam carriages and fire-engines.

American inventors were early on the scene with "gas-buggies," even before Daimler (whose engines were built by Steinway, of piano fame, under licence in Long Island from 1891 to 1896) or Benz had exhibited their cars at the 1893 Chicago World's Exposition. First in the field, apparently, was John W. Lambert, of Ohio City, whose three-wheeled car was running in January or February 1891. Also in 1891 Henry Nadig, of Allentown, Pennsylvania, built a four-wheeled car with an 8-h.p. single-cylinder engine, which with an 1893 two-cylinder engine installed was in use until 1903, and still exists today, as does the 1892 Schloemer from Milwaukee. In September 1893, Charles E. Duryea and his brother Frank were operating a car in Springfield, Massachussetts; they began production in 1896. Later, Duryea were the first American petrol car manufacturers to bring their products to Britain: a depot was opened near Cannon Street.

Frank Duryea's *Times-Herald* racer, 1895

British Pioneers

At the end of the 1880s Frederick Bremer, a young cycling enthusiast from Walthamstow, London, had the idea of fitting a gas engine to a bicycle to save pedalling. It was not until 1892, however, that he began work on a motorcar, at the age of 19. The diminutive Bremer car was probably completed in 1894, and owed much to Karl Benz' patents. Primary transmission was by fast-and-loose belts, giving two forward speeds, and final drive was by chains. The single cylinder, made from an iron pipe, was laid horizontally under the seat. The inlet valve was automatic. Like the Benz, the crankshaft was exposed, with oilers to lubricate the bearings. Ignition was electric, by trembler coil, and Bremer made his own sparking plugs with pipeclay insulation. Bremer ran the car very little, and almost always after dark to avoid brushes with the law.

About the same time as Bremer, John Henry Knight of Farnham, Surrey, designed a petrol car. He had built a steam vehicle in 1865, and now owned the Reliance Motor Works, builders of stationary engines. Their foreman, George Parfitt,

Bremer car, 1894-95

The first Lanchester car 1895-96

supervised the construction of a three-wheeled car with a rear-mounted $2\frac{3}{4}$-h.p. single-cylinder engine capable of 500 r.p.m. It was first tried on the road in May 1895, and was later converted to a fourwheeler.

Around 1893 a young engineer named Frederick Lanchester was designing flying machines, but, being convinced that their time had not yet arrived, he then began work on a motor car, helped by his younger brother George. The car, which first ran in early 1896 was, perhaps, the most advanced and original vehicle then built. The steering, controlled by a balanced tiller, was properly laid out with castor and camber angles to keep the car moving in a straight line at speed: no other designer had paid serious attention to steering geometry. The tubular space frame was exceptionally rigid, and the single cylinder engine had electric ignition, a mechanically operated inlet valve and two contra-rotating crankshafts.

In 1895, Sir David Salomons held an open-air display of imported horseless carriages at Tunbridge Wells, Kent. The first indoor exhibition of cars in Britain was at the Stanley Cycle Show, November 22-30, 1895, where the public was also introduced to the moving pictures, in the form of the Edison Kinetoscope. Five cars were shown, including a l'Hollier (Benz), a Gladiator "mineral naphtha" tricycle, a "Facile" heavy-oil carriage from the Colchester firm of Britannia, and the Hon. Evelyn Ellis' Daimler, in which the future Edward VII had his first petrol car ride in 1895.

Emancipation Day

Harry J. Lawson was an extremely gifted engineer. In 1879, aged 27, he was working at the Rudge Co., in Coventry, and there built the first chain-driven safety bicycle. In 1881 he patented and apparently built a gas-engined bicycle. Lawson was also an astute if not over-scrupulous businessman who realised very early on that the motorcar was the coming thing, and determined that he alone would control the industry. He therefore bought up the English rights to the patents of the leading Continental manufacturers; then, by intensive publicity, educated the British public as to the prospects of the motor industry, and finally launched automobile manufacturing companies with capitals totalling millions of pounds. All this needed talent of a very special order, for cars were still restricted to 4 m.p.h.: but Lawson, backed by the notorious Terah Hooley's funds, had that talent.

His first launch was the Daimler Motor Co. (which built very inferior Panhard-Levassor copies) in January 1896: they were housed in the four-storey Motor Mills at Coventry. Most of Lawson's many companies ended in liquidation in the early 1900s; his patent monopoly was proven worthless, and he was

sentenced to 12 months' hard labour for his financial chicanery.

After repeated lobbying, Parliament agreed to raise the speed limit to 12 m.p.h. Lawson decided to celebrate with a run from London to Brighton on Saturday November 14, 1896. Unfortunately for posterity, this run was very inaccurately reported in the motoring press. Most of the successful cars seem to have been of Panhard, Bollée or Benz pattern, although the first "heavy car" to reach Brighton was apparently one of the two Duryeas specially brought over from America – the other, which ran over a little girl at Crawley, came in eighth. The weather was terrible, fog and rain predominating, and several of the cars were surreptitiously sent down by train to ensure their arrival at the finish. Journalists enthused about "rushing through the air at the speed of a torpedo-boat destroyer" but top speeds were probably around 20 m.p.h.

"It is too early to predict the extent to which horses may be displaced by motor carriages" commented Sir Herbert Maxwell, Bart., "but it can scarcely be doubtful that their obvious imperfections will yield to the ingenuity of inventors so as to render them at least dangerous rivals to the old kind of equipage." Those were bold words indeed for 1896.

Mayade's Panhard and the Daimler landau *Present Times* leaving the Hotel Metropole, London, at the start of the Emancipation Day run

De Dion and Bouton

It was December 1881. The 25-year-old Count De Dion, one of the most celebrated young aristocrats in Parisian society, was strolling down the Boulevard des Italiens, looking for cotillion favours for a ball, when his attention was caught by a little model steam engine worked by spirits-of-wine in the window of a toy-shop. Always keenly interested in mechanics, he bought the engine, and asked the shop-keeper, Giroux, who had built it. "Georges Bouton," came the reply, "who works with this brother-in-law Trépardoux in the Passage Léon". The two, who built toy engines for Giroux and *modèles de vitrine* (showcase models) for the precision engineering firm of Ducretet, earned very little, and were easily persuaded to enter into partnership with the wealthy De Dion to build steam cars.

At the 1889 Paris Exhibition De Dion was impressed by the internal-combustion engine, and he and Bouton designed and built a 12-cylinder rotary two-stroke. Trépardoux was bitterly opposed to this new development: he was the "brains" of the company as far as steam was concerned, and designed the "De Dion" boiler and the "De Dion" final drive. Despite his protests, De Dion and Bouton continued the development of petrol engines, and even disposed of some of their designs to Merelle, who produced light De Dion-type threewheelers under licence – so in 1894 Trépardoux, thoroughly piqued, left the company, thereafter known as De Dion Bouton.

In 1895 the first successful De Dion Bouton petrol engine appeared. It was an air-cooled one-cylinder four-stroke of $\frac{3}{4}$ h.p. (50 × 70 mm., 134 c.c.) and ran at the hitherto unprecedented speed of 2,000 r.p.m. (it even reached 3,500 r.p.m. on test, but could not sustain this). At first, De Dion engines were fitted into speedy tricycles, which made a great name for themselves in competition, and power units also were built in various capacities to be sold to car and motorcycle builders; detachable cylinder heads formed part of the specification.

In 1889 a rear-engined $3\frac{1}{2}$-h.p. voiturette was added to the De Dion range, and in 1901 the output of its single cylinder engine was raised to $4\frac{1}{2}$ h.p. The next year a complete revision of the design was undertaken, and the 6-h.p. engine was housed under a fashionable "crocodile" bonnet.

De Dion steam tricycle 1883

1¾-h.p. De Dion tricycle and Belvalette trailer

1000-Mile Trial of 1900

In 1900 the Automobile Club of Great Britain and Ireland (which became the Royal Automobile Club in 1907) inspired by Claude Johnson, the Secretary (who was later *eminence grise* of Rolls-Royce), decided to organise a demonstration of motoring which would bring home the reliability and efficiency of the automobile to as many people as possible: at that time there were still a great many who had never even seen a car. A 1,080-mile route was mapped out to pass through the major cities of England, and it was planned that the competing vehicles would be exhibited at the Agricultural Hall, Islington, before the event, *en route* at Bristol, Birmingham, Manchester, Edinburgh, Newcastle-on-Tyne, Leeds and Sheffield, and at the Crystal Palace after the trial was over.

Competitors were supplied with a list of "Petroleum Spirit Stores" – cycle works, car manufactories, chemists and ironmongers – of whom there were only 41 in the entire distance, but were warned that orders should be placed early, and that "the Agents will not, in many cases, accept orders unless accompanied by a proper remittance, owing to the expense to which they are often put to by having spirit ordered from them, but subsequently not called for."

The Austin designed 1,000-mile trial 3-h.p. Wolseley

The first Napier car

At 7 a.m. on Monday, April 23, the competitors began to leave London from Hyde Park Corner: first stop was 3½ hours later, for breakfast at Calcot Park, near Reading, country home of Alfred Harmsworth, one of motoring's staunchest supporters. That day's run ended at Bristol: the next day the vehicles were exhibited in aid of the Transvaal War Fund. During the Trial, the cars were timed for efficiency in hill-climbing on Taddington Hill; Shap Fell (optional); Dunmail Raise and the ascent from Moffat to Birkhill, and a limited number of the competitors was tested for speed on a private road on the Duke of Portland's estate at Welbeck Park. Far and away the fastest car was the Hon. C. S. Rolls' 12-h.p. Panhard, which averaged 37·63 m.p.h. over a measured mile; second, at 29·6 m.p.h., came the very first Napier car, the 8-h.p. phaeton owned by Edward Kennard, and driven by S. F. Edge, co-director, with Harvey Du Cros (of the Dunlop Rubber Co.) of the Motor Power Co., which provided Napier's backing.

Surprisingly few of the 67 competitors retired, and most of those that did drop out did so from minor causes, although the Motor Manufacturing Co.'s tricycle was withdrawn as "new frame and wheels were substituted at Manchester, and a new motor was fitted to frame at Nottingham."

The First Sports Cars

Early in 1896 Léon Bollée, already famous for having constructed an advanced calculating machine at the age of 19 in 1889, introduced a light tricar, which unlike other small cars of the period, was exceptionally speedy. Moreover, this *voiturette* was the first car to be produced with pneumatic tyres as standard. Its low-slung appearance contrasted strangely with the four-square cars of the day, and aroused much controversy. Writing in *La Nature* on May 16, 1896, L. Baudry de Saunier remarked: "The elongated form of the tricycle, redolent of speed, gives it somewhat the semblance of a little torpedo-boat, and whoever has seen it shoot by at 50 k.p.h. on the level will recognise that the nickname already given it of *'torpilleur de route'* is justified". Low-priced and idiosyncratic, the Bollée voiturette enjoyed a brief vogue before it was superseded by better, more practical designs.

Among those motorists whose desire for speed was kindled by ownership of a Bollée tricar was Emil Jellinek, a wealthy Austrian. In May 1897 he ordered four cars from the Daimler Motoren Gesellschaft, specifying that they should be capable of 40 k.p.h. (25 m.p.h.), a speed regarded by the Daimler directorate as only attainable by express trains. Then Jellinek pressed for an even more powerful car, with a four-cylinder engine mounted in front; he ordered six, and set his talents to work to sell them, as Baron Henri de Rothschild recalled in a lecture in 1903: "In 1899 I was at Nice with my uncle, Baron Arthur de Rothschild. Climbing La Turbie hill one day on an 8 h.p. Panhard, we were passed by an enormous motorcar which had more the characteristics of an elephant than a gazelle, and got to the top of this long gradient some time before us. This easy victory rather ruffled my uncle, who prided himself on possessing the fastest car turned out at the time. He sought the owner of the car and proposed to buy the vehicle. The bargain was immediately concluded, and my uncle descended La Turbie with the car which had beaten him on the up-grade". The driver of the car, a 12-h.p. Daimler weighing $1\frac{1}{2}$ tons, was, of course, Jellinek.

A fortnight later, the Rothschilds were again motoring up La Turbie, once more Jellinek passed them. So Baron Arthur acquired another Daimler. Later Jellinek persuaded the Roths-

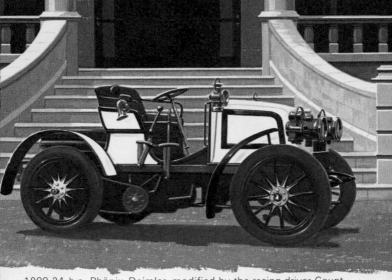

1900 24-h.p. Phönix-Daimler, modified by the racing driver Count Eliot Zborowski

childs to become the first customers for the new 24-h.p. Phönix-Daimler, which was "by no means elegant, but the price was certainly proportionate to the weight".

Mercedes

Although the 24-h.p. Phönix-Daimler was fast – maximum speed was around 45 m.p.h. – it was unwieldy, and dangerous on corners. Emil Jellinek was aware of this, and wanted a car built on entirely new lines, "the car of the day after tomorrow." He tried to persuade Wilhelm Maybach, the talented chief of design at Daimler, to leave them and head a new company which Jellinek proposed to set up in Paris with financial aid from Vanderbilt and Rothschild, but without success. Then Wilhelm Bauer was killed when his Phönix-Daimler went out of control in a competition at La Turbie, on March 30, 1900. This gave Jellinek the lever he needed. He signed an agreement to take over the sales of all Cannstatt-Daimlers of more than 8 h.p., and told Maybach to design a 35 h.p. car "comparable with no other". If the car was entirely to his satisfaction he would order an entire series (36 cars). The new

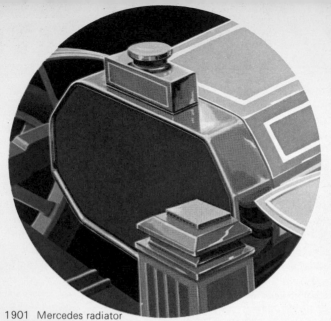

1901 Mercedes radiator

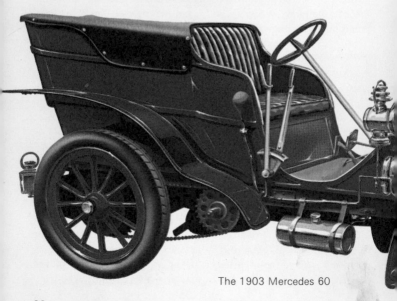

The 1903 Mercedes 60

model was to be named after Jellinek's daughter, Mercédès.

Early in 1901 the Mercedes was unveiled. Although recognisably descended from the Phönix-Daimler, it combined many features for the first time: a honeycomb radiator, a pressed steel frame, mechanically operated inlet valves, low-tension magneto ignition and a selective "gate" for gear changing. Long and low, the Mercedes "set the fashion to the world". Its debut, at the Pau race meeting of February 17, 1901, was marred by teething troubles, but at the Nice Week (March 25-29) Mercedes cars swept the board. In 1902 came the vastly improved "Mercedes-Simplex", which truly threw off all vestiges of the horseless carriage – it became evident that the 40 h.p. Mercedes-Simplex was the fastest petrol car of its size in the world when Baron de Caters covered a flying kilometre at Ostend at a speed of some 75 m.p.h.

In June 1902 Jellinek ordered a new model, rated at 60 h.p. with a 9,236 c.c. engine with overhead inlet and side-exhaust valves. Firm orders for 60 of these cars were received almost immediately. First shown in the spring of 1903, the new 60 h.p. was blindingly fast for a production car, exceeding 80 m.p.h. with racing bodywork, and represented the high point in the collaboration of Maybach and Jellinek, who changed his name to Jellinek-Mercédès in its honour.

Racing 1895-1905

On July 22 1894, the Parisian newspaper *Le Petit Journal* sponsored a reliability trial for horseless carriages over an 80-mile course between Paris and Rouen. Of 102 entries, only 26 were ready in time for the event, and seven of these failed to survive the eliminating tests. But the trial, in which the first prize of 5,000 francs was won jointly by Panhard and Peugeot, was a great success, and led to the setting up of a committee (which became the Automobile Club of France) to organise a proper race over the 732-mile Paris-Bordeaux-Paris course in June 1895.

Its purpose was to prove speed and reliability; to discourage the very fastest cars, it was stipulated that the first prize would only be awarded to a vehicle with more than two seats. This proved somewhat embarrassing as the first two cars home were both two-seaters, Levassor's Panhard and Rigoulot's Peugeot, so first prize was awarded to Koechlin's Peugeot, the third car to arrive, eleven hours after Levassor.

Levassor had driven the entire distance single-handed, with

1895 Paris-Bordeaux Panhard

1899 Bollée *torpilleur*

only one involuntary stoppage of 22 minutes apart from scheduled halts for petrol and water, and had thus remained at the tiller of his car for some 48 hours 48 minutes, even driving through the night by the light of candle and oil lamps. His average speed for the journey was 15 m.p.h. This event really proved the superiority of the petrol car, especially in unskilled hands, for though six of the 22 starters were steamers, and one electric, the first eight cars to finish (spread out over 34 hours) were petrol-driven, while the ninth (and last) was an 1880 Bollée steamer which limped in two days later.

The speed of racing cars began to rise, and as a consequence, accidents happened. In the 1,062½-mile Paris-Marseilles-Paris contest held between September 29 and October 4, 1896, the list of casualties was alarming. Bollée No. 20 ran into a tree blown down in a storm, while Bollée No. 21 was attacked by a bull; Panhard No. 7 tried to avoid a stray cart, smashed a wheel and threw its passengers out, badly injuring one; the crew of the Rossel (No. 28) were resting after pushing it up a steep hill when a gust of wind sprang up and blew it back down again to destruction; while Levassor, driving Panhard No. 5, hit a dog and overturned, receiving internal injuries which hastened his death the following year.

The Paris-Marseilles-Paris race was won by Mayade's 8 h.p.

A typical racing Stanley, Louis Ross' lethal-looking *Tea-Kettle*, gets away from the petrol-powered opposition on Daytona Beach, 1905

Panhard, with the new four-cylinder engine, at a speed of 15·7 m.p.h.

As the century neared its end, many of the racing cars taking part in the leading events bore crude attempts at streamlining. For the 1897 Paris-Trouville, ex-racing cyclist Ferdinand Charron endowed the boxy prow of his Panhard with an aggressive beak, while in 1898 Amédée Bollée junior astounded the racing world with his "aggressive but speedy" *torpilleurs,* which boasted scientifically designed wind-cutting aluminium coachwork, and produced exceptional speed from an engine of only 8 h.p., giving the Panhards their first serious competition. In 1899 Bollée constructed four *torpilleurs* especially for the 1,350-mile Tour de France, with a mechanical layout decades ahead of their time. These cars had independent front suspension by double transverse springs; "double steering"; a strongly made steel channel chassis frame which passed *under* the rear axle; a rear-mounted air-cooled 20 h.p. horizontal four-cylinder engine with all four cylinders cast in one block for the first time ever, and twin carburetters. Oddly out of place were the four-speed belt drive, hot-tube ignition and automatic inlet valves – but these were features common to many 1899 cars. Once teething troubles had been overcome, the cars proved capable of over 90 k.p.h.; but in the race road-dust sucked in by the rear-mounted carburetters (and hasty preparation) caused their engines to break down and only one completed the course, in 5th place.

The year 1899 also saw the appearance of perhaps the most famous of the first generation of streamlined speed cars, *La*

Jamais Contente, the invention of the red-bearded Belgian inventor Camille Jenatzy, who later became the top Mercedes racing driver. *La Jamais Contente* was driven by a powerful electric motor on the back axle, and had the smallest wheels (shod with pneumatic tyres) that had then been used on a car; this was to give the most favourable gear ratio. The coachwork of the car, shaped like a bullet, and built of *Partinium* (the first aluminium alloy made in sheet form) could have been the work of Jules Verne; it was in fact the product of the celebrated Parisian carriage-building firm of La Maison Rothschild. Jenatzy had built this car for the sole purpose of defeating the speed of 39·3 m.p.h. set up at Achères, not far from Paris, over 2 kilometres from a standing start by the Count de Chasseloup-Laubat's electric Jeantaud. On April 1, 1899, four days after *La Jamais Contente* had been completed, Jenatzy attempted to break Laubat's record, but the timekeepers were not ready, and though he claimed to have succeeded, his car had to be towed away ignominiously to have its Fulmen batteries recharged. Four weeks later Jenatzy again took *La Jamais Contente* to Achères, rushed along the 2 kilometre course "with a subdued noise like the rustling of wings . . . scarcely seeming to touch the ground", and recorded the phenomenal speed of over 105 k.p.h. (65·75 m.p.h.) over the flying kilometre, which record he retained for three years.

The next major step forward, 100 *miles* an hour, did not come until July 17, 1904, when Rigolly, driving a monstrous 15-litre Gobron-Brillié, with a four-cylinder, opposed-piston engine (two pistons per cylinder), exceeded 100 m.p.h. in the standing start mile and flying kilometre during Automobile Week at Ostend. Even this brave attempt is overshadowed by the amazing steam-driven Stanley *Rocket,* which in January 1906 touched 127·66 m.p.h. on Ormond Beach, Florida. The next year, at a speed estimated, no doubt optimistically, at 197 m.p.h., the *Rocket* became airborne and disintegrated. The driver, Fred Marriott, was lucky to escape alive.

During 1899, James Gordon Bennett, the millionaire proprietor of the *New York Herald,* was cruising in the Mediterranean in his palatial steam yacht, the 2,000-ton *Lysistrata.* A motoring enthusiast since 1893, Gordon Bennett was turning over in his mind a scheme he had conceived for an international motor racing trophy. He announced his intentions in October, and a set of rules was drawn up in consultation with the Automobile Club de France. Chief among these was the stipulation that the prize was only to be raced for by the official representatives of clubs recognised by the A.C.F. These were the Automobile Clubs of America, Austria, Belgium, Germany, Great Britain & Ireland, Switzerland and Turin, each of which

Charron's 1900 Gordon Bennett Panhard

was empowered to nominate three drivers and three cars for the race, scheduled for June 14, 1900.

The drivers for the French team were chosen by ballot, which occasioned a good deal of bitterness, for the three selected – the Chevalier René de Knyff, Charron and Giradot – were all Panhard drivers, while the Mors drivers who had done so well in competition during 1899 were either made reserves or omitted entirely. Other countries, far from having to cast a ballot to select their teams, were hard put to find anybody to represent them: only Belgium, Germany and America came forward.

The 354-mile course, from Paris to Lyons, was an obstacle course rather than a speed track, the drivers suffering from obstreperous gendarmes, flocks of sheep, and worst of all, dogs – every driver is said to have killed five or six. Charron drove over a cross-gutter too fast, and bent his back axle badly. He decided to continue, his mechanic, Fournier, pouring oil over the strained driving chains. Ten miles from the finish, speeding downhill at 60 m.p.h. he hit a St. Bernard, which lodged between the wheel and the steering arm, completely jamming the steering. The car shot off the road,

This horizontally-engined 96-h.p. Wolseley Beetle was raced by C. S. Rolls in the 1905 Gordon Bennett

jumped the ditch, rushed between two trees, across a field, between two more trees, and finished up on the road again, facing the wrong way. The water-pump having been knocked off, Fournier had to lean out and hold it against the flywheel, but they won, cheered on by the smallest crowd ever to watch the end of a major race. "There were at least a dozen people", remarked the lugubrious Charron.

The next year, Fournier drove for Mors and won the Paris-Berlin, the season's major event.

As the speed of racing cars rose, it became more and more apparent that long distance races between cities posed many problems, not least of which was the policing of spectators, who would crowd into the road to watch the approaching cars. In addition, control zones had to be set up where the course passed through cities. Things were rendered even more hazardous in 1902, when the heavy racing cars in the Paris-Vienna were limited to an overall weight of 1,000 kilogrammes (2,210 lb) with an extra 7 kg. allowed for a magneto, with no restriction on engine capacity. Panhard hastened to take full advantage of this, and constructed a team of 70 h.p. racers in which everything was subordinate to lightness and power. The engine was a 13·8-litre four, developing 70 b.h.p., and the car complete weighed 19¼ cwt. Tests proved that the frame was a little weak, and all the Paris-Vienna Panhards were modified in this respect, except that of the British driver Charles Jarrott. During the race, Jarrott's frame did break, and he mended it with string and wood from a bed, smuggled out of his hotel in his trousers. Other team 70 Panhards, driven by Henry and Maurice Farman (the aviation pioneers), Teste and Pinson, came in first, third, fourth and fifth in their class.

After Paris-Vienna, Jarrott thought that his Panhard would be an ideal car in which to set up the fastest time ever registered in England, at the forthcoming Welbeck Speed Trials. The snag was that the car was still in Vienna, unrepaired, and the Panhard company showed little interest in repairing it in the near future. Then Jarrott's team-mate Pinson suggested that the best plan would be to enter for the forthcoming Circuit des Ardennes, the first closed-circuit race, organised over a 53-mile triangular course in rural Belgium – then Panhard would be certain to overhaul the car. Jarrott not over-keenly agreed and Panhard rebuilt the car. At Bastogne, the starting-point, Jarrott found that the cars were to start in numerical order, irrespective of engine capacity, and that he had been drawn 32nd. Never having driven on the course,

Jarrott's 13·8-litre 70-h.p. Panhard, 1902

he stood little chance, especially as No 1 was the favourite, Baron Pierre de Crawhez, organiser of the race, whose first lap was covered at 57·1 m.p.h. from a standing start on his 70 Panhard. The course was exceptionally dusty, and the slower cars constituted a great hazard – one by one the faster drivers crashed. De Crawhez knocked off both front wheels while passing Coppée's Germain, while Jenatzy went into the ditch upside down on his 60 h.p. Jenatzy, his wheels landing on the far side of the road. Baron de Caters hit a wall with his Mors, while a report affirmed that Théry's light Decauville *"est entrée dans une vache, et y reste."*

Jarrott, driving at his superb best, roared steadily through the field until at half-distance only Gabriel's Mors was ahead of him. For the remainder of the race, Jarrott lay just behind the Mors – then, just over 4 miles from the finish, he saw Gabriel pull up suddenly with a broken driving chain. Jarrot swung past and went on to win what proved to be his only victory in a distinguished career of racing.

The next week, in pouring rain, he convincingly shattered the Welbeck record, covering the flying mile at 64 m.p.h.

The great race of 1903 was to be over a course from Paris to Madrid, and promised to be the finest event of its kind ever

Gabriel's Paris-Madrid Mors *Dauphine*

1903 Gordon-Bennett Napier K5

organised. The entry list closed with 216 cars and 59 motor-cycles down to start on May 24 over a course of some 840 miles. The 1000 kg. limit was still in force, and the Paris-Madrid *grandes voitures* represented the apotheosis of power and lightness.

The race attracted some three million spectators, most of whom were quite unused to racing cars, and the *Services d'Ordre*, who were supposed to be holding back the crowds, "served . . . merely as additional crowds, specially privileged to stand in the middle of the roads at all danger points. The result was a double line of human hedges scarcely two metres apart, between which one was asked to race at upwards of 80 m.p.h.", complained a Mors driver. The day was swelteringly hot, and blinding dust was thrown up from the untarred roads by the cars, so that drivers had to steer by the treetops.

Small wonder there were fearful accidents, and that over

Lancia's 1905 Vanderbilt Cup FIAT

half the competitors fell by the wayside. The race was halted by Government edict at Bordeaux, where the winner was announced as Gabriel, whose Mors *Dauphin* had covered the 342 miles from Paris at the fantastic average of 65·3 m.p.h. Ironically, shortly before the race, Gabriel had tried to get out of his contract with Mors to drive one of the new 90 h.p. Mercedes, but the German company had been unwilling to pay the 20,000-franc compensation fee due to Mors if Gabriel left them.

The days of city-to-city racing were over; henceforth closed circuits were to be the rule.

Six weeks later, the Automobile Club of Great Britain & Ireland organised the best Gordon Bennett of the series. S. F. Edge had won the 1902 event, run concurrently with the Paris-Vienna, on his 40 h.p. Napier, and the British rushed through a Bill enabling them to hold the race in Ireland. The race was won by Jenatzy, driving a borrowed 60 h.p. Mercedes, as the team of 90 h.p. Mercedes prepared for the race had been destroyed in a holocaust at the Cannstatt works. As the 90 was demonstrably inferior to the 60, this was no doubt a blessing in disguise.

While American racing car designers in the early part of the century showed remarkable originality of thought, their products lacked staying power. W. K. Vanderbilt, Jr., one of America's richest men, and a notable amateur competitor in European events at the wheel of a 70 h.p. Mors, decided to remedy that situation by sponsoring a race on his home ground. The first Vanderbilt Cup Race, held on October 8, 1904, over a triangular course on Long Island, attracted German, French, Italian and American entries. As in the European races, crowd control proved an almost insuperable task, and the rough surface of the course, which was traversed by half-a-dozen level crossings took a savage toll of the competing cars. George Heath, the popular American driver, just managed to keep his 90 h.p. Panhard ahead of Albert Clément's 80 h.p. Clément-Bayard in the last lap to win by $2\frac{1}{2}$ minutes – and then the crowd swarmed on the track and the race was stopped.

The 1905 Vanderbilt Cup was won by Victor Hémery (80 h.p. Darracq), closely followed by Heath (120 h.p. Panhard).

In 1904 and 1905 the Gordon Bennett was won with ease by Leon Théry (Richard-Brasier) but the A.C.F. were disenchanted with the Gordon Bennett regulations, which allowed France, the leading car producing nation, only three entries. It was decided that the Gordon Bennett should be abandoned. In its place the A.C.F. would organise a new race – the Grand Prix.

Théry's 1905 Gordon Bennett Richard-Brasier

Coupé trois quart on the forward-control 20cv chassis; the coupé body is by Muhlbacher

Body Styles

In the early years of this century, an amazingly diverse number of body styles was available. This continued to be the case until the advent of the flush-sided torpedo touring body just before the Great War. These illustrations show some of the fashionable styles of 1905; all these examples were available from one company, Charron, Girardot & Voigt, a partnership of famous racing drivers, with works at Puteaux (Seine).

Coupé by Muhlbacher on the 18cv chassis paid no heed to the comfort of the chauffeur, but was undeniably elegant

The *cab* body by Muhlbacher on the 20cv chassis was only slightly more weatherproof than an open tourer

Among the more remarkable designs to emanate from this firm were one of the earliest straight-eights, an early armoured car and a gigantic 12·9-litre model with geared-down starting handle (chauffeurs must have been getting soft!): one of these – with a built-in lavatory – is preserved at the headquarters of the Veteran Motor Car Club of America. At the other end of the scale, many early London taxis were twin-cylinder Charrons with landaulette coachwork.

A more intimate *coupé* by Labourdette on the 18cv chassis; the spider seat at the rear would accommodate, uncomfortably, a footman

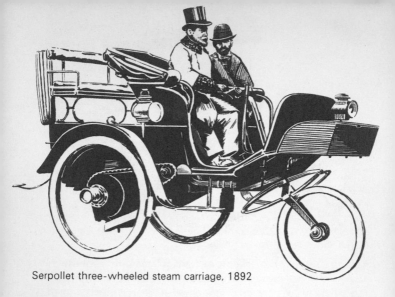

Serpollet three-wheeled steam carriage, 1892

Steam Cars

One of the paradoxes of motoring history is the easy victory of the petrol motor over the long-established steam engine. In the early days steam appeared to have all the advantages, yet by 1910 it was virtually extinct as a motive force, except on some heavy commercial vehicles. It has, even today, many devotees who would like to see a modern steam car in production; such attempts, however, always seem to end in failure. In the long history of the steam car, one man stands out as having given the petrol car the nearest run for its money. He was Léon Serpollet, the son of a blacksmith of Culoz (Ain), France. Around 1875, aged 17, Serpollet made a major step forward in steam technology with the invention of the flash boiler, in which water, pumped into a red-hot serpentine iron pipe, was instantly converted into superheated steam. This meant that steam was only generated as it was needed in the engine, and a boiler explosion was impossible, as there was so little steam in the boiler at any time. The only major precedent was the American John McCurdy's "Patent Steam Chamber" of 1824.

In 1887 Serpollet set up in business in Montmartre, where

he constructed a steam tricycle, which incurred police displeasure until it had passed a road-worthiness test. In 1889 a three-wheeled car was built to Serpollet's design by the Beaulieu bicycle factory of the great Peugeot ironmongery company, in which Serpollet and Ernest Archdeacon made an epic 290-mile trip from Paris to Lyons, which took around a fortnight, and during which 350 lb. was added to the car's starting weight of 1,200 lb. by repairs. Serpollet found a rich, if limited, clientele for his cars, and a number was produced during 1890-91.

Serpollet's financiers, thinking the motorcar a wild fancy, forced him to concentrate on building steam-trams during the 1890s, and it was not until he met Frank Gardner, a wealthy American who offered to back him, that he could once again give his attention to cars. Gardner and Serpollet entered into partnership in 1898, and the next year the first Gardner-Serpollet paraffin-fired twin-cylinder cars were on the market.

Léon Serpollet's aim was to make a steam car as easy to start and control as a petrol vehicle, and he certainly succeeded – but they remained more complex to build and service.

In 1901-02, Serpollet racers were the fastest cars in the world, and Mercedes almost acquired rights to produce a Mercedes-Serpollet. Control on the later Gardner-Serpollets

The fastest car of 1902
Serpollet's sprint car
Easter Egg

Locomobile steam Stanhope model O3, 1901: Kipling called his a 'nickel-plated fraud'

was almost automatic, and they could be started from cold in six minutes.

Unhappily, Léon Serpollet died of consumption at the early age of 44 in February 1907 and the company died with him.

If France led the world in the design of steam cars, the United States certainly had pre-eminence in their production, and the genus lived on there well into the 1920s. One of the earliest was the Stanley, built from 1896 at Newton, Massachussetts, by the identical twin Stanley brothers, Francis E. and Freelan O., who had made their fortune in 1895 by selling the rights of their patent photographic dry plate to Eastman Kodak. In 1899 they sold their design to the Locomobile Co., for $250,000 and undertook to abstain from making cars for two years. The Locomobile steamer was mass-produced on a scale then unique, 4,000 being turned out in under three years, at a time when there were only some 8,000 cars running in the U.S.A. A huge depot was set up in South Kensington, London, where "Locomobiles were bought like eggs", and the type enjoyed a brief vogue in Britain. But though steam could be raised "in less time than it takes to harness a horse and carriage", the Locomobile was too frail to be a continued success, and had a tendency to commit *suttee* if left standing with the burner lit. By 1903 the Locomobile company had dropped steam in favour of petrol; meanwhile the irrepressible Stanleys had returned to the market with a new design omitting all the snags of their original model, and Stanley Steamers remained in production until 1927.

Perhaps the best of the American steam cars was the White, introduced in 1901, and unique among its compatriots in featuring a flash boiler. From its inception the White was successful in reliability trials, hill climbs and races.

The 15 h.p. White of 1905 offered more refinement and silence for £550 than any contemporary petrol car; it had a twin-cylinder compound engine which could be "simpled" to give extra low-speed torque, could run 150 miles on one filling of fuel and water, had aluminium coachwork and in addition to direct drive had the unusual refinement of a two-speed back axle giving an emergency low gear and neutral, so that water and fuel pumps could be run while the car was standing, eliminating hand pumping. Top speed was around 50 m.p.h. President Taft favoured the "Incomparable" White, but even such distinguished patronage proved insufficient to keep sales at an acceptable level, and after 1910 the steamer was supplanted by a petrol car, which was popular in Tsarist Russia.

1905 15-h.p. White

57

Electric Cars

As we have seen, early racing motorists used battery-electric cars for one furious burst of all-out speed – apart from Jenatzy and Chasseloup-Laubat, there was Baker in America, whose submarine-shaped speedster of 1902 featured safety-belts for the tandem-seated occupants, and in Britain the remarkable *Toujours Contente* built by the Luton firm of E. W. Hart in 1900. Capable of 50 m.p.h., it had a Lohner-Porsche motor in each hub, making it probably the world's first four-wheel-drive car.

Even in touring form battery range was restrictive, and recharging could be expensive. An electric car costing £700 could cost as much again in annual running costs, and hiring it on a contract basis was no cheaper. But to a limited market, the electric was the ideal car. "If you use your carriage simply for shopping and making calls or going for short drives, or for driving a short distance to business every day, *and for nothing else,* then I advise you to buy an electromobile, which of all town carriages is the most luxurious and convenient", wrote Filson Young in 1906 – while adding warningly: "But for any other purpose the electric carriage is the least useful

Electric racer: Hart's *Presque Contente*, 1901

and most expensive form of motor-car".

Large fleets of electric cabs were plying the streets of London and Paris at the turn of the century, yet by 1910, like steam cars, the breed was virtually extinct. In America, however, where to venture outside the city limits could be a hazardous operation on the quaggy roads, the electric enjoyed a much longer security of tenure, and was employed in all sizes from light two-seat runabout cars to huge urban delivery trucks of 5 or 7 tons capacity. Most American electrics were off the market by 1925, but the Anderson Electric Car Co. continued to offer their celebrated Detroit Electric against special order until 1939.

Another category of electric cars used a normal petrol engine to drive a dynamo generating power for the electric motors. The earliest example was the Mercedes-Mixte of 1907, designed by Porsche, and a later example was the 1920 Owen Magnetic from America, billed as the "Car of a Thousand Speeds"; two were built in Britain as "Crown Magnetics" by the British Ensign Car Co. – one before, one after the company went bankrupt. The petrol-electric transmission was really too heavy for a normal car – its true metier was in the field of passenger transport, where the best-known user was the Maidstone, Kent, firm of Tilling-Stevens.

Popular Motoring

In the early days of motoring, it took a rich and dedicated enthusiast to use a car as regular transport, for there were few places where fuel could be obtained, ignition arrangements were less than reliable and the early pneumatic tyres were unable to stand up to the weight of the car on terrible road surfaces for long. Moreover, the police and magistrature were openly hostile.

Society was turned topsy-turvy, for the policeman was now empowered to arrest the rich man to whom he had always previously shown deference, should he observe him breaking the speed limit. It was only human nature that some policemen should abuse this power. Traps were set and motorists who were timed to cover a set distance at more than the legal limit (unless altered by local by-laws, 12 m.p.h. from 1896 to 1903,

'If the scout fails to salute, STOP and ask the reason'

The reason . . . 1905 Prosper-Lambert falls into the trap

20 m.p.h. from 1904 on) were taken to court. The accuracy of these speed traps was generally open to doubt, for cheap imported stopwatches were used, and the method of marking the measured distance was often ludicrous: in one instance, two cabbage leaves laid on the road served this purpose. Policemen concealed themselves in hedges and ditches: my favourite headline of the period runs "CONSTABLE UP A TREE. REMARKABLE EVIDENCE IN ARUNDEL MOTOR CASE".

Surrey was especially "antimotorist", and loomed large on the weekly map of current speed traps published in *The Autocar*; their prize trapper was Inspector Jarrett of Chertsey, who brought so many motorists to court that he gained promotion from Sergeant to Inspector in one year (1904-5). It was to combat police traps that the Automobile Association was founded in 1905: their bicycle-mounted scouts gave members advance warning – "If a scout fails to salute, *stop* and ask the reason". On one celebrated occasion an AA scout was arrested on a charge of perjury for stating in court that a member could not have exceeded the limit, as the scout, on his bicycle, was keeping pace with the car *uphill*: the 300-strong AA staked their all on this case and won, despite the hostile summing-up given by the judge and false testimony of the police witnesses. Membership increased apace from then on, and at the Olympia Motor Show of 1906 the 5,000th member was enrolled. Only five years later, the AA, now with 19,513 members, absorbed the older-established Motor Union, with its 8,527 members.

Motoring in the days before the Great War could, nevertheless, be pretty adventurous, as things still went wrong *en route,* and the pioneer motorist had to be quite an ingenious roadside mechanic. For example, the log of a round trip from London to Stratford-on-Avon (around 240 miles in all) in 1907, on a 16/20 h.p. Brown with a Forman engine, ran as follows: "Left London 5 a.m. First stop 20 miles out – sheared key on camshaft. New one fitted, then all was well to Stratford. Next day, left Stratford 5 a.m. Ball race in gearbox failed, new one fitted. Universal joint fell to pieces, new one fitted. Four punctures (about 10 spare inner tubes always carried as well as the Stepney spare). Just outside Oxford a big end and con rod came through the base chamber. Set to work taking all the bits out and eventually got going on three cylinders with a

Popular British car –
1905 Rover 8

piece of rag in the hole in the base chamber.

"Purchased several gallons of oil. My job was to keep putting oil in the lubricator under the dashboard, and, believe it or not, our run home from Oxford on three cylinders was the best of the whole journey, and we arrived home at 5 a.m. the next morning".

A pioneer lady motorist recalled some of the hazards of those days for me: "There was no traffic problem: in a drive of 30-40 miles, one encountered only four or five cars, but there were hazards on the roads. Engines were noisy, horses unaccustomed to cars were frightened and restive. One came on hay waggons piled high, the carter perched on the shafts asleep, roused suddenly by the car's horn, flustered and uncertain which way to go.

"Children had a dangerous game of last across to see who would be last to race in front of an advancing car. Dust was a danger, too: I have had to stop and wait, completely blinded by a cloud raised by a passing car driven fast. Dogs rushed out, barking furiously; chickens fluttered, terrified, under one's wheels; vehicles held the crown of the road. I recollect following a traction engine for some considerable distance. Its driver was unable to hear our hooting due to the noise of his machine. At last I had to run to overtake it, and attract the driver's attention to tell him that our car desired to pass".

Popular American car — 1903 'curved-dash' Oldsmobile

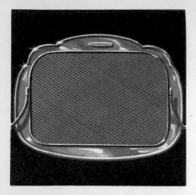

The Face of the Car

Some radiator designs of typical marques of 1906.

LÉON BOLLÉE: In limbo after the three-wheeled 1896 voiturette went out of production, the Léon Bollée name was revived in 1903 for a range of Vanderbilt-financed quality cars (Baron Henri de Rothschild backed a similar project in 1902 under his pseudonym 'Pascal'). In 1924 the Léon Bollée factory at Le Mans was acquired by Morris Motors

DELAUNAY-BELLEVILLE: Long famed as boiler makers (hence the circular radiator and bonnet) the French firm of Delaunay-Belleville built their first car in 1904. They were of superb quality, and an enthusiastic owner of several Delaunays was Nicholas II, Czar of all the Russias

ITALA: Founded in 1903, Itala made their name with their racing successes, and were Italy's largest manufacturers after FIAT in Edwardian days. In 1912 Itala introduced a model with rotary valves serving both for intake and exhaust: it was not in production long

HELBE: Built by Levêque et Bodenréder (L et B = Helbé) at Boulogne-sur-Seine, the Helbé was an assembled car using De Dion engines and some Delage components. It is said that the Austrian Puch car was based on the Helbé

PANHARD LEVASSOR: After inspiring car design in the pre-Mercedes era, Panhard settled into a period of refined conservatism, then, in 1912, they adopted the Knight sleeve-valve engine for many of their models. These *Sans Soupapes* Panhards were quiet, refined — and smoky

TURGAN: In its original (1899) form, known as the Turgan-Foy, this marque from Levallois-Perret (Seine) featured the weird twin-cylinder, double-vertical-crankshaft Filtz engine. Later designs were more orthodox, but by the end of 1906 the firm's output was entirely composed of commercial vehicles — petrol tramcars were a speciality

Luxury Motor Cars

"That most elaborate and costly form of luxury, the high-powered, sumptuously fitted motor-car, which as a means of travel has in the few years of its life eclipsed the railway train in speed, comfort and convenience" attracted a surprising number of adherents in the days before the Great War, people who could afford to spend £1,500 to £3,000 on a car *and* bear annual runnings costs of £700 or more, 50 per cent of which would be tyre replacements and repairs. Up till 1906

Governed to 20 m.p.h. and silent as an electric — the unsuccessful V8 Rolls-Royce Legalimit, 1905

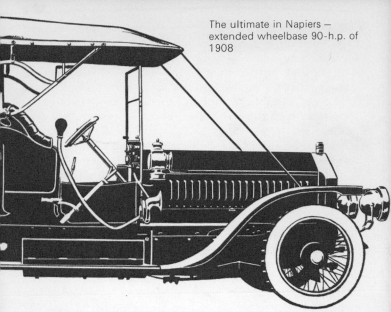

The ultimate in Napiers — extended wheelbase 90-h.p. of 1908

the leading make was Mercedes, strongly challenged by a number of very fine cars – De Dietrich, Itala, Panhard, Renault, Mors among others – and in 1903 a new factor was added to the choice of a high-class motor when the English firm of Napier announced their new 18-30 h.p. six-cylinder model. The first Napier "six" was bought by W. Bramson: "It was rather a brave thing to do", claimed S.F. Edge, who controlled Napier sales, "but . . . he never regretted his courage in having done so".

Edge was a remarkable personality who lost no chance of promoting the Napier image, by competition successes, endurance runs, or the voluminous correspondence he maintained with the motoring press. He always maintained that "six cylinders was the perfect combination", but early six-cylinder design often left much to be desired, for designers had insufficient understanding of the problems of carburation and crankshaft balance. Before the invention of the crankshaft damper, six-cylinder cars were beset by sudden attacks of *delirium tremens* as the critical engine speed at which periodic vibration occurred was reached, and it was not unknown for crankshafts to shear in two from this cause. The ebullient Edge, however, was equal to this problem: it was not harmful vibration that one felt on the Napier cars, he claimed, but an innocuous phenomenon known as the "Power Rattle." The length of the engine on early six-cylinder cars seems to have posed a problem; Napiers, especially, had a nose-heavy appearance, which was belied by their precise handling qualities.

Mercedes managed the "six-cylinder look" with far more aplomb than most, and their 1908 75 h.p. model was a car of surpassing beauty, especially when fitted with a two-seated sporting body – a *folie de grandeur* of the highest order. But by the time this car reached the market, the infant firm of Rolls-Royce, after experimenting with two-, four- and six-cylinder models of 10, 20 and 30 h.p. respectively, had introduced their new 40/50 h.p. six-cylinder model.

The 40/50 h.p. Rolls-Royce engine kept vibration to a minimum by the combination of a massive crankshaft and unfashionably "square" engine dimensions (bore and stroke 114 × 114 mm.) in an era of long-stroke power plants. The entire car was beautifully constructed and its solidity bore witness to Henry Royce's early training as a locomotive engineer.

Inspired, perhaps, by the example of the Hotchkiss Co., which had started a 45 h.p. six-cylinder Hotchkiss on a 15,000 mile trial – the longest distance recognised for an R.A.C. certificate – throughout the British Isles on April 29, 1907,

Grahame-White's extended wheelbase 75-105-h.p. Mercedes, 1913

Baron von Eckhardstein's six-wheeled De Dietrich, 1903

Rolls-Royce arranged a similar test of the 40/50. Between June 21 and August 8 the 40/50 known as *Silver Ghost* (C. S. Rolls named several of the "works" cars: the earliest such was *Grey Ghost,* a 20 h.p. four shown at the 1904 Paris Salon) covered 15,000 miles with only one involuntary stop, apart from tyre troubles, when, after 629 miles the petrol cock vibrated shut, and caused one minute's delay. According to the certificate issued by the R.A.C., labour costs during the test totalled £16 13s. 7½d.; repairs, replacements and renewals came to £11 11s. 5d. Tyres, at £12 0s. 9d. for a front cover and tube and £13 5s. 9d. for a rear tyre and tube, came to a total of £187 12s. 6d., and the total cost of running the car over the 15,000 miles was £281 8s. 4½d., or approximately 4½d. per mile. The Hotchkiss, which didn't finish its trial until August 20 (and thereby had its thunder stolen by the Rolls-Royce), spent only a quarter as much time being repaired (9 hr. 44 min. as against 40 hr. 13 min.) but used the astounding number of 46 tyres during the trial at a cost of around £550. The Rolls-Royce results caught the public fancy, for the car was proved durable and silent as well as elegant, and the "Silver Ghost" type toppled Mercedes from the position of "The Best Car in the World".

There was a class of purchaser, however, to whom mere elegance was not enough: ostentation had to be added to it. Perhaps the most fantastic example of this was the De Dietrich built for Baron von Eckhardstein in 1903. The Baron had

Elegance by the yard — the extraordinary 1910 Gregoire triple berline

sworn to eclipse the magnificent Panhard Pullman Limousine de Voyage owned by his rival Count Boni de Castellane, which had a 12 ft. 6 in. wheelbase, hot and cold running water to a silver washbasin, electric lighting and heating, and every conceivable instrument on the dashboard. Von Eckhardstein's car, said to have cost £4,000, or in the region of five times as much as a standard De Dietrich of the same horsepower (35), had six wheels, the extra axle being positioned in the middle of the chassis. The passengers were carried amidships in a compartment richly furnished by Maple & Co., while the rear of the car was occupied by a kitchen, in which a chef prepared meals *en route*.

It became established early on that the length of the bonnet was an important factor in the design of the high-powered motorcar: only the idiosyncratic Lanchester brothers and their imitators placed the engine between the front seats to give as much passenger room as possible. As in the 1930s, a long bonnet might be an utter sham, concealing a miniscule engine, but conversely, a big Edwardian engine would need the maximum of space: sumps two yards long were not uncommon. In 1906, if you were so minded, you might purchase complete for £1,500 a 60 h.p. Leader, the product of an obscure Nottingham firm, which had an eight-cylinder engine of 127 mm. bore and 153 mm. stroke: cubic capacity was 15·5 litres, almost certainly the largest eight-cylinder power unit ever fitted to a production car. This was remarkably cheap compared with the contemporary 90 h.p. Napier, which at a chassis price of £2,500 in 1907 (£1,000 less the next year!) offered a mere $14\frac{1}{2}$ litres, and about on a par with the 1907/8 Ariel-Simplex 50/60 h.p. six, which offered 15·9 litres for £950 (chassis only).

The Leader wasn't the first eight-cylinder car to be built, for Charron, Girardot and Voigt had constructed one in 1902, which dispensed with the gearbox, having only two speeds – forwards and backwards.

Another fine car which eliminated gear-changing was the six-cylinder 45 h.p. "gearbox-less" Sheffield-Simplex of 1909-12, which did the majority of its travelling in direct drive, although an"emergency low" gear also was incorporated in the back axle. A handsomely bodied example of this model ran successfully from Land's End to John O'Groats entirely on direct drive. Other unusual features of the Sheffield-Simplex were an accelerator pedal that pivoted sideways, and a single pedal to operate both clutch and brake.

It also featured that most delightful Edwardian eccentricity, a circular radiator and bonnet, which it had in common with France's greatest luxury car of the period, the Delaunay-Belleville. The latter make pioneered pressure lubrication of crankshaft bearings, and had as its proud slogan "The Car Magnificent". Delaunay-Bellevilles were favourites of the Czar of Russia, and a hint of their excellence can be gained from this description of one of their exhibits at the 1911 Olympia Show: "The features of this Limousine-Landaulette

Czar's choice – the Delaunay-Belleville. A 1911 37-h.p. tourer by D'Ieteren Frères

body by D'Ieteren Frères are the absence of all the unsightly ironwork usually associated with a Landaulette, and the wonderful finish of the interior, painted violet clair. The interior fittings, roof and sides are of polished Amaranth of a peculiarly deep mauve colour".

Some very fine cars were produced in America in the late Edwardian period: perhaps the most distinctive was the Pierce-Arrow, built by the George N. Pierce Co., of Buffalo, N.Y. Available with 36, 48 and 66 h.p. six-cylinder engines, the Pierce-Arrow had cast aluminium coachwork fitted on an ash framework and, from 1913, the famous "fender headlights", although conventional lamps could be had as an option. As Pierce advertising claimed in the 1920s "the owner is never embarrassed by having his car mistaken for any other make", and there were few takers for the more mundane headlamp placement: President Woodrow Wilson was one of the exceptions. He was also the first resident of the White House to favour the Pierce – the last was Franklin D. Roosevelt.

At a lower price level, the 20/30 Cadillac of 1913 offered remarkable value for money. Extensive use was made of electricity, for in 1911 the company had been the first to offer

Luxury V8 – the
1915 Cadillac

Inside the 1917 Packard Twin-Six

electric lighting and starting as standard, which by eliminating the starting handle attracted many women to learn to drive. It was advertised, somewhat ominously, as the "Self-Starting Self-Igniting and Self-Lighting Cadillac", but its principal novelty was a dual-ratio rear axle also actuated by electricity. In 1915 Cadillac introduced a V-8-engined model (the first V-8 cars were the 1903 Paris-Madrid racers built by Clément Ader, in 1890, the first man to leave the ground in a heavier-than-air flying machine in his steam aeroplane *Eole*), but even this was overshadowed by the announcement the same year of the V-12 Packard Twin-Six. In 1913 the British Sunbeam company had been producing V-8 and V-12 aero-engines, and a V-12 racing car, *Toddles V*, took many records at Brooklands. On the outbreak of war, a Sunbeam V-12 engine was sent across to America, and gave Jesse G. Vincent the inspiration for the Twin-Six, and the Liberty aero-engine. The Twin-Six was produced until 1924, when the Single-Eight replaced it.

One American venture into multi-cylinders which had unforeseen results was the decision in 1907 by the Chadwick Company of Philadelphia to build an 11½-litre six based on their 7⅔-litre four-cylinder model. A single carburetter was used, and gas distribution was so terrible that the top speed was only 65 m.p.h., less than the smaller four-cylinder model's maximum. Willie Haupt, who supervised construction of Chadwick's racing cars, fitted three carburetters, one to each pair of cylinders. This gave an immediate increase in top speed of 20 m.p.h., but Haupt wasn't yet satisfied, and began experiments with forced induction, and racing Great Chadwick Sixes had a supercharger which gave a top speed of over 100 m.p.h.

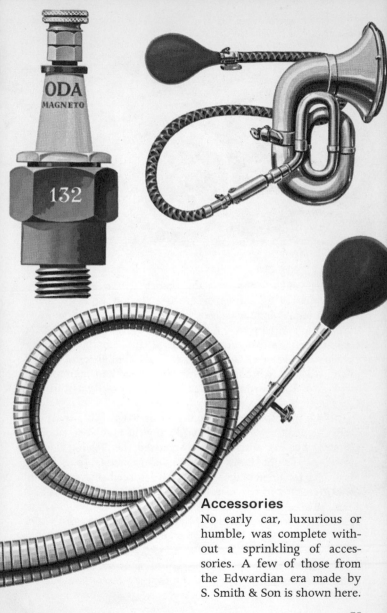

Accessories

No early car, luxurious or humble, was complete without a sprinkling of accessories. A few of those from the Edwardian era made by S. Smith & Son is shown here.

Duray (De Dietrich) saves his mechanic on the Hairpin Turn — an exciting incident of the 1906 Vanderbilt

Racing 1906-14

The big event of 1906 was the French Grand Prix, the race which was to take over from the Gordon Bennett in the international calendar. It was held on two consecutive days, Tuesday and Wednesday June 26-27, and run over 12 laps of a triangular 64-mile course near Le Mans. Entries were received from France, Germany and Italy, but Britain, piqued at the way the Automobile Club de France had manoeuvred the end of the Gordon Bennett, had temporarily withdrawn from international racing.

For the first time, only the driver and his riding mechanic were allowed to work on the car during the race, instead of the teams of helpers who had characterised the Gordon Bennett series. A weight limit of 1,000 kilogrammes (plus 7 kg. allowance for a magneto) was strictly enforced, and most of the 32 cars to start in the race were perilously close to the upper limit. Three of the teams – FIAT, Bayard-Clément and Renault – employed the new Michelin detachable rims, which greatly simplified tyre-changing at the expense of a little extra weight.

At 6 a.m. the cars began to be sent off at 90-second intervals, and there was some danger of the first starters coming round before the last few competitors got away. By the end of the third lap, halfway mark for the day, the Hungarian driver Szisz (Renault) had taken the lead from Baras (Brasier). All through the first day the red Renault led, and when the cars were locked away overnight, Szisz was 26 minutes ahead of the next man. Epic feat of the day occurred when Le Blon ran off the road near St. Calais and buckled the right rear wheel of his Hotchkiss. He immediately set about rebuilding it, using spokes borrowed from the other wheels of the car, and from the car of his team mate Salleron. Three hours later he was back in the race, but retired before the day was out. The weather was extremely hot, and tyre troubles were rife: this showed the advantages of the detachable rim for tyre changing – but the detachable wheel was still a thing of the future.

On the second day, the cars were sent off at the intervals at which they had finished the evening before. There was no catching Szisz, who led throughout the day's racing, finishing half-an-hour ahead of the young Italian Felice Nazzaro's FIAT, and averaging 63 m.p.h. over the 769·9 mile course.

European cars and drivers competed in force in the 1906 Vanderbilt Cup, which was led from start to finish by Wagner's 110 h.p. Darracq. Again the race had to be stopped after the first few cars had arrived because crowds flocked on the track as they had in 1904 and 1905.

Ferenc Szisz won the 1906 Grand Prix on this Renault.

The motor racing world was electrified by the news that Hugh Locke King, a wealthy motoring enthusiast, was to build a vast track on his Brooklands estate, at Weybridge, Surrey. His aim was to enable the British motor industry to try out its products in high-speed competition, away from the stifling 20-m.p.h. speed limits in force on the highways. Work on the track was begun in the autumn of 1906, and a cheerfully pagan army of Irish labourers moved in to clear the site and lay the concrete. In six short months, Brooklands was complete at a cost of almost £250,000. The circuit, roughly egg-shaped, was almost 3 miles long, and at either end the 100-foot wide track was swept up into concave bankings over 20 ft high, round which cars could travel at over 100 m.p.h. without undue strain.

On June 28-29, 1907, before the track was officially opened, S. F. Edge, in an unprecedented feat of endurance, averaged 66 m.p.h. for 24 hours at the wheel of a 60-h.p. Napier, setting up a new world record which remained unbroken for years.

The opening meeting took place on July 6 1907, and a full programme of races was held. But only 4,000 spectators turned up; the vast size of the track dwarfed the cars; the Press, half of whom had received no free passes, were openly hostile; the cars were unnumbered (the drivers wearing coloured "jockey" smocks instead) and so it was impossible accurately to follow the progress of a race, and, worst of all perhaps, the cars were unhandicapped, so the race always went to the swiftest machine. The takings at the gate might have just been enough to buy one of the many elaborate trophies given that afternoon.

It took a year to put things right and the real turning point in the story of Brooklands was the appointment of A. V. Ebblewhite as timekeeper to the Brooklands Automobile Racing Club in June 1908. "Ebby" introduced numbering for the cars and, more important, established a system of handicapping based on observed lap speeds.

Any lingering doubts about the effectiveness of Brooklands as a spectacle were dispelled at Whitsun 1908, when a much publicised three-lap match race for £250 a side between Nazzaro on his 90-h.p. FIAT *Mephistopheles* and Frank Newton on the bullet-nosed 90 Napier *Samson* was run off. The Napier soon took the lead, but on the third lap its crankshaft broke – a victim of the celebrated "Power Rattle" – and Nazzaro roared

A. V. Ebblewhite ('Ebby') starts the final of the Sprint Race at the Grand Motor Meet at Brooklands, May 28, 1910 — at this time drivers still wore jockey smocks in distinctive racing colours. Below is a plan showing the track as it was when opened: the Finishing Straight slices across the Outer Circuit

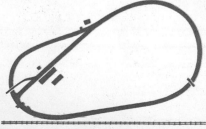

by to win. The speeds for the second lap were the cause of a controversy that has never quite died down, for the new electrical apparatus gave the FIAT's lap speed as a record 121·64 m.p.h., the first two-mile-a-minute run in England. But "Ebby", timing by hand, said the FIAT had only reached 107·98 m.p.h.: and Ebby was invariably right.

Apart from the opening of Brooklands, motor racing in 1907 was dominated by the remarkable achievement of Felice Nazzaro in winning three major races – the Targa Florio, the Kaiserpreis and the French Grand Prix. What made this accomplishment even more outstanding was the fact that all three of these races were run under different formulae, and though Nazzaro's mount in each case was a FIAT, the engine capacities were 7·4, 7·8 and 16·25 litres respectively.

The other prominent event of 1907 was the Peking to Paris "race", across some of the most inhospitable terrain in the world. Two De Dions, an Itala, a Dutch Spyker and an unlikely

Bogged down in Siberia – the New York-Paris Thomas Flyer

cyclecar called a Tri-Contal started on June 10, and all finally reached Paris except the Tri-Contal. The winner was the 40-h.p. Itala driven by Prince Scipione Borghese, which reached Paris on August 10, but the contest proved the impossibility of driving from Peking to Paris – an army of 150 coolies was needed just to get the cars out of China!

Not in the least daunted, *Le Matin,* the Paris newspaper which had organised Peking-Paris, planned an even more ambitious contest for 1908, in conjunction with *The New York Times*. This was to be a 20,000-mile race from New York to Paris, no less! The route was to be: New York to Alaska, via Chicago, San Francisco and Seattle, then across the Behring Straits ("always frozen in the winter") under their own power or on sledges, to Vladivostok; then across Asiatic Russia to Irkutsk, Moscow, Berlin and Paris. Few serious entries came in: there were four from France (De Dion, Sizaire & Naudin, Motobloc and Werner), one each from Germany (Protos),

Italy (Brixia-Züst) and America (Thomas-Flyer).

The trans-American trip, through snow, slush and mud, showed up defects in all the competing cars. By San Francisco, only the Thomas, Züst, De Dion and Protos were still in the race. The Thomas-Flyer was shipped to Valdez, Alaska, where the snow was so deep that the only way the car could cross Alaska was piecemeal, on sledges at a cost of $10,000.

The route was then changed, and the Thomas, De Dion and Züst travelled via Japan to Vladivostok, to catch the Protos.

All through the race the Thomas was plagued by transmission trouble; this let the Protos into the lead at Omsk. Alarmed by the prospect of a German car winning the race, the organising committee fiddled the rules and kept publicity

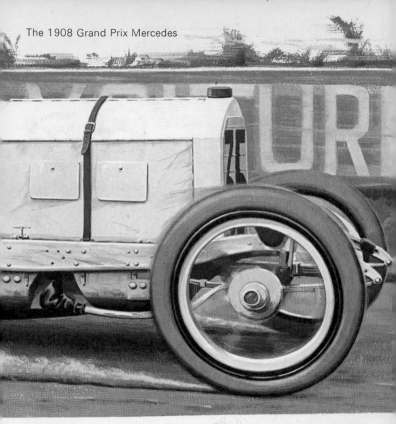

to a minimum. When the Protos entered Paris it was met with blank stares. After much wrangling, the Thomas was declared the winner by 26 days on elapsed time.

The 1908 French Grand Prix was held on July 7, over ten laps of the 47·8 mile Circuit de la Seine-Inférieure, which had been used for the 1907 race. A new formula had been drawn up, combining a minimum weight of 1,100 kilogrammes with a maximum piston area of 117 sq. in. (R.A.C. rating 59·6 h.p.), which at the existing state of engine design meant an output of around 100 b.h.p.: but the Bayard-Clément and the British Weigel companies improved on this figure by using inclined overhead valves in a hemispherical combustion chamber, operated by a single shaft-driven o.h.c. The Bayard-Cléments

The 30-litre 300 h.p. Fiat racer

developed some 135 b.h.p. from 13·963 litres, and one was clocked at 105·1 m.p.h. over a kilometre during the race.

The period preceding the race was clouded by a dispute between S. F. Edge and the ACF, which resulted in Edge refusing to enter his Napier team, because the GP rules forbade the use of the Rudge-Whitworth detachable wheels with which they were fitted: wheels were reckoned to be part of the car, and not to be replaced during the race. (Edge did gain some racing kudos, though, in the 1908 Isle of Man Tourist Trophy, for the Hutton car which won was really a four-cylinder Napier. Edge made sure that everyone realised this by entering the Huttons in his own name, rather than that of Jack Hutton.)

In the Grand Prix, the dominant factor was the unreliability of the new type of Michelin detachable rim, which was located by a single bolt where eight had served before: among those eliminated by this cause was Szisz (Renault), the victor of the 1906 G.P. The race was a virtual walkover for Germany, being won at an average of 69 m.p.h. by Lautenschlager, whose Mercedes was, however, running on the last set of tyres left in its pit when it finished. Second and third were Benz cars.

The French motor industry, unable to stomach its defeat, proposed a ban on all motor racing, and many of the leading firms were signatories to this ill-considered document.

Brooklands was invaluable to the British motor industry, for it was the only place in the British Isles where cars could be tested to their limit. Those manufacturers who appeared most frequently at the track made the most highly regarded cars of the day from the viewpoint of efficiency – Vauxhall, Star, Sunbeam, were especially distinguished. Even the leading foreign manufacturers sent over cars for record-breaking attempts: Fiat built a monstrous 30-litre Brooklands 300-h.p. car which Bordino brought over to the track in 1913, and "Cupid" Hornsted was renowned for his feats with his two "Big Black" Benz cars. These were really painted a very dark blue, Hornsted's old bicycle-racing colour, and the first of them, which arrived in London in January 1912, was a 15,095-c.c. four with pushrod o.h.v. Despite its bulk, it "steered like a dream." It could lap Brooklands at 105 m.p.h., yet was so tractable that Eric Horniman (of the tea family) went on honeymoon in it. It was, however, eclipsed by the 200-h.p. Benz which came to England in the autumn of 1913 with instructions to go for all the world's records possible. This had a 21·5-litre engine, and direct drive on top gear giving 140 m.p.h. at 1,400 r.p.m. It broke world's records 27 times, culminating in a new land-speed record of 124·1 m.p.h.

But the most famous record to be established at Brooklands was set up on February 15, 1913, by Percy "Pearley" Lambert, driving an extensively streamlined 25-h.p. Talbot of 4,531 c.c. Lambert had already covered a mile at 111·73 m.p.h. in this car the previous November. Now he was out for the most coveted record of all, the hitherto unbroken 100 miles in the hour. Lapping steadily high up the banking, "Pearley" covered 103 miles 1,470 yards in 60 minutes.

Percy Lambert's 100-mile-in-the-hour Talbot

The decision of the majority of the French manufacturers to withdraw from Grand Prix racing after 1908 was, in the long run, of great benefit to the development of the motor car, for attention was thereby thrown on racing voiturettes, and much was learned about the design of small high-speed engines. The principal event in the Voiturette calendar was the Coupe de l'Auto, initiated in 1905. At first the rules, which imposed a limit on the bore, encouraged the development of freakish long-stroke engines, the apotheosis of which was reached in the 1908 Lion-Peugeot, with its 3-ft. tall engine and the exhaust pipe passing over the top of the driver's head. The rules were altered in 1908 to include light four-cylinder engines, and the harvest of this was reaped when Zuccarelli won the 1910 Coupe on his Hispano-Suiza, trouncing Goux' Lion-Peugeot; Chassagne was third on another Hispano.

1912 Grand Prix: Peugeot and Sunbeam on the Dieppe circuit

1914 Grand Prix Mercedes

In 1911, too, an attempt was made by the Automobile Club de l'Ouest to revive the Grand Prix. A motley entry of voiturettes and antique GP racers was received, and the "Grand Prix de Vieux Tacots (Old Crocks)" as the press sneeringly called it, was won by Hémery on a 10-litre Fiat. Remarkably, second place was taken by a 1,327-c.c. Bugatti driven by Friderich.

In 1912 the Automobile Club de France decided to hold a "genuine" Grand Prix: playing safe, they combined it with the popular Coupe de l'Auto, and, as in 1908, ran it over the Dieppe circuit, of which 10 laps were to be covered on two consecutive days. The crack Peugeot drivers Georges Boillot, Jules Goux and Paul Zuccarelli had collaborated with a Swiss engineer, Ernest Henry, to produce a new type of racing engine, with four cylinders *en bloc,* twin overhead camshafts, operating four inclined valves per cylinder, and central plug location: it was blatantly cribbed by engineers the world over. At 7·6 litres, the Peugeot was one of the largest cars in the race, the last of the old giant racers being epitomised by the 14-litre Fiats and 15-litre Lorraine-Dietrichs. Boillot won the race, despite major transmission trouble.

In 1913 Boillot won the Grand Prix by $3\frac{1}{2}$ minutes from Goux: a strong challenge from Guyot (Delage) evaporated when he ran his mechanic over during a wheel-change.

The legend of the invincibility of Boillot and his Peugeot was dispelled when the Mercedes of Lautenschlager, Wagner and Salzer took first three places in the 1914 G.P. at Lyons.

The New Motoring

It may have been the influence of the Coupe de l'Auto, or merely the desire to own a small cheap car with a reasonable speed potential – whatever the reason, around 1910 enthusiasts began constructing tiny *bolides* powered by motorcycle engines, often ignoring established conventions of design and with potentially lethal top speeds. In the vanguard of the "New Motoring" movement, as it became known, was the Bédélia, designed by Robert Bourbeau, assisted by his friend, H. Devaux, in 1910. Long and narrow, the Bédélia had two seats in tandem: the driver sat and steered from the rear. The steering column was connected to the ends of the front axle by steel cables: the axle pivoted in the centre, like that of a cart, a totally indefensible arrangement which had last been used on the hopelessly retrograde Clément-Panhard of 1899. Two speeds forward were available, if the passenger shifted the inordinately long driving belts between pulleys of different diameter with a long piece of wood, and the tubular petrol tank was carried immediately above the aircooled engine, in just the right position to create a merry blaze if it should leak – which was not at all unlikely. But because of its high power-to-weight ratio, the Bédélia proved popular with impecunious sportsmen, and soon full-scale production was under way in Bourbeau's little factory in the Rue Félicien-David in Paris.

A more practical design was the Morgan, the prototype of which was constructed in 1909 by H. F. S. Morgan, a young

Longest-lived cyclecar – the Morgan in 1931 Super Sports form

motor agent of Malvern, Worcestershire. Powered by the V-twin engine from a crashed Peugeot motorcycle, the Morgan tricar was an ingenious machine in which the propeller shaft was carried down the tubular chassis backbone, which had a spider to support the engine/clutch assembly at one end and a bevel box brazed on at the other. From this box emerged a shaft, carrying at either side a chain sprocket. These gave different ratios, being engaged by dog-clutches, and drove to a single rear wheel, which bore the only brake, a notably inefficient wrap-around band affair. Front suspension was independent, by sliding pillars. The Morgan three-wheeler survived until 1948, when the supply of sporting V-twins dried up.

Another cyclecar which featured dog-clutch engagement of sprockets of differing sizes to give the different speeds was the GN, built by H. R. Godfrey and Archie Frazer-Nash in Hendon from 1910. This was a fourwheeler: most GNs made prior to the Great War had belt final drive, like contemporary motorcycles.

The *annus mirabilis* of the New Motoring was 1912: the annual Cycle and Motor Cycle Show at Olympia had the suffix "and Cyclecar" tacked on, while Temple Press Ltd. introduced *The Cyclecar,* a penny weekly, of which over 50,000 copies were put on sale. At the Show, 40 different makes of cyclecar were on display, ranging from the Rollo Monocar at 70 guineas to the Eric at 135 guineas. The latter was a chunky-looking tricar with spindly axles, a tubular space frame, an under-floor 1088-c.c. horizontally-opposed twin-cylinder engine in unit with a three-speed and reverse gearbox and shaft and bevel drive to the rear wheel. Already the crude early cyclecars such as the Bédélia were beginning to look out of date, and the coming thing was obviously the "big car in miniature," represented at that 1912 show by the £125 twin-

An early belt-drive GN

The Bébé Peugeot

cylinder Swift, modestly described by the makers as "the one thing that was needed to complete Motor History," and the 848-c.c. Wilkinson, built by a company better known today for swords and razor-blades. This had the water-cooled engine with four separately-cast cylinders and three-speed and reverse gearbox fitted to the advanced Wilkinson TMC motorcycle. Friction drive, which remained popular while power outputs were low, was featured on the Girling, the GWK and the Surridge Cyclar.

The old-type cyclecars had a field day in July 1913, however, when a Grand Prix des Cyclecars was held at Amiens. W. G. McMinnies, of *The Cyclecar* came in first, on his Morgan, three minutes ahead of Bourbeau's Bédélia: but the French declared that the Morgan was a motorcycle and sidecar, and that the Bédélia had obviously won the cyclecar prize. But nobody took any notice.

One of the best of the early light cars was the Bébé Peugeot, designed by a young Italian engineer named Ettore Bugatti who had just set up in business on his own account in Molsheim, Alsace. It had a monobloc four-cylinder engine of 856 c.c.

and a novel two-speed transmission using two crown wheels, and two pinions on the ends of two concentric propeller shafts.

Slightly larger was the 1096-c.c. Singer, with a three-speed gearbox integral with the rear axle. Lionel Martin, of Bamford & Martin, motor engineers, bought one at Olympia 1912. He was looking for a high-performance light car as a foil to his Rolls-Royce Silver Ghost, and by the use of special camshafts, achieved over 70 m.p.h. This Singer was so successful in competition, especially at the Aston Clinton hillclimb, that it inspired Martin to build his own car in 1913, using an Isotta Fraschini chassis and a Coventry Simplex engine. This hybrid was christened "Aston Martin".

Of all the cyclecar companies, only GN and Morgan long survived the war building cyclecars, but one of the earliest in the field, AC, began in 1913 to make handsome 10-h.p. Fivet-engined light cars with a bullnosed radiator like the contemporary Morris. Their original Auto-Carrier of 1907-14 was an eccentric tiller-steered tricar based on the company's motorised tradesmen's box van: at £95 fully equipped, the

1915 Singer 10

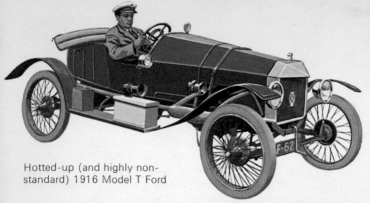

Hotted-up (and highly non-standard) 1916 Model T Ford

Auto-Carrier was good value for money. But the 10-h.p. four-wheeler, especially in sports form, laid the foundations for the firm's halcyon days in the 1920s under the direction of S. F. Edge, who had parted with Napier after a dispute in 1912 for the colossal "golden handshake" of £160,000, on the understanding that he would keep out of the motor business for seven years. So he went in for pig-farming in a very successful way until after the war.

In 1913, the New Motoring even attempted to make its mark in America. Among its staunchest advocates was W. H. McIntyre of Auburn, Indiana, who built a tandem-seated cyclecar called the Imp, with all-round independent suspension by parallel transverse leaf springs, friction transmission, and final drive by belts some 16 ft. long overall. But

1913 Imp Cyclecar

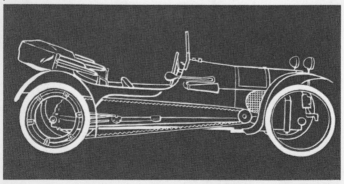

by 1914 the Imp was out of production: it was quite obviously not the car for American roads, which were at that period generally atrocious. Few roads even boasted a token topping of gravel, and in the rainy season the dirt tracks turned into quagmires. A cheap car intended for inter-urban transportation had to be rugged, with a good ground clearance, which the Imp obviously was not. It suffered the same fate as the Brush Runabout of 1908, the unorthodox construction of which was caustically summarised as: "wooden body, wooden axles, wooden wheels, wooden run".

Better roads were on the way; in 1913 the Lincoln Highway Association was founded to press for a proper transcontinental

1913 AC 10

road across the USA, but new legislation in 1916 provided for federal aid to improve road systems, and the Association was disbanded. Until the new roads were built, rural America was to place its trust in the Model T Ford, the go-anywhere, do-anything, any-darn-fool-can-drive-it car introduced in 1908 by Henry Ford, who applied sound marketing and long-established techniques of mass production to producing a car for Everyman. He succeeded so well that from a first cost of $850 in 1908, when 5,986 Model Ts were sold, the price had fallen to $550 by 1913, when 182,809 people bought Fords (and by 1916 the figures were $360 and 577,036).

93

Some Oddities

Although the basic layout of the motor vehicle was established very early on, there have always been inventors and designers who for some reason or another have sought to flout convention. These are some of the more outrageous or eccentric of their confections.

(1) The multiple axles of the 1912 Reeves Octoaulto were supposed to give a smoother ride on rough roads; (2) This little 1902 Dunkley was designed to run on coal gas and could be filled from lampposts. The firm later built motorised prams; (3) The 1912 Wolseley Gyrocar ran on two wheels, steadied by a gyroscope; (4) In 1897 M Joseph Mille patented this design for a petrol tractor with electric starting; (5) In 1912 the Brooke Car Co. built the 'Car that hisses like a swan' for an eccentric Englishman resident in Calcutta.

1

2

Sporting Cars

It is extremely difficult to say exactly when the true sports car came into existence – the first recorded use of the term was in August 1900, when the ephemeral Sports Motor Car Company, of South Kensington, London, unveiled the twin cylinder Sports Car, capable of averaging 35 m.p.h. over the atrocious roads of the period. I think the deciding factor is the point at which high speed ceased to be the prerogative of gigantic engines in scanty chassis, and scientific design began to play a part. The beginnings of this movement were to take place in Germany where the royal family were ardent motorists. Kaiser Wilhelm, inaugurator of the Kaiserpreis, had started with a Phönix-Daimler in 1900: his brother Prince Henry of Prussia was a long-time Benz fan. Inspired by the Herkomer Trophy Trials for touring cars held from 1905 to 1907, Prince Henry offered a prize for four-seated touring cars, with bores restricted to minima of 85 mm. (fours) and 69·6 mm. (sixes) and maxima of 146·5 mm. and 120 mm.

The results were not quite what he intended, for many of the competing cars in the first Prince Henry Trial, held in 1908, were little more than four-seated racing cars with the most

A 1914 Prince Henry Vauxhall

rudimentary mudguards and bodywork. The event was won conclusively by Fritz Erle, driving a Grand Prix Benz with light touring coachwork.

Traditionalists were horrified by the low-slung, futuristic, bodies of the Prince Henry cars, quite unlike the conventional upright *Roi des Belges,* which seemed to rise in tiers from a low bonnet. So for 1909 the rules of the event were recast to eliminate the "freaks" and the result was a very dull contest.

In 1910, Prince Henry tried again. A minimum body width at the top of the doors was stipulated, to discourage the "racers in touring trim". But nothing was said about the width of the lower part of the body, so many of the German competitors fitted bodies which flared sharply inwards from the top, to reduce frontal area. This style was copied by German coachbuilders for many years, and was the inspiration for some of the most hideous bodywork ever.

A young designer named Ferdinand Porsche, who had just joined Austro-Daimler, determined to win the 1910 Prince Henry, and produced a team of special cars with engines derived from his earlier work on the power units of the Parsifal airship. Porsche *did* win, and his team-mates took

English-bodied 1912 27/80-h.p. Austro-Daimler

second and third places. The "Prince Henry" Austro-Daimler became a production model, as did the Pomeroy-designed Vauxhalls which had run through the event with notable reliability.

What were those first sporting cars like to drive? Certainly they had little in common with the modern sports car, for they were not designed for shattering acceleration. In those days tyre bills were heavy enough without shortening tyre life even further by furious driving. Top gear flexibility was highly prized, and the intermediate ratios were merely an aid to climbing steep hills.

To enter such a car, you climb in from the passenger side, for entry from the right is baulked by the gear and brake levers (most high class Edwardians, no matter what their nationality, have right-hand steering). If, as is likely, the car has Bosch dual ignition, you will have turned the engine over compression a

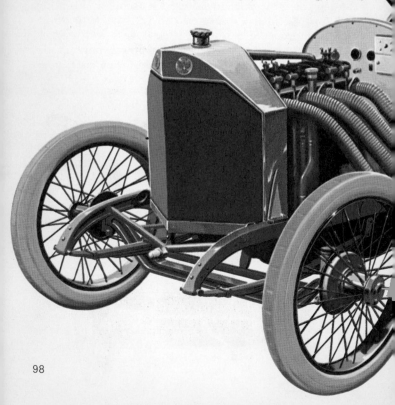

few times to prime the cylinders with gas-air mixture. Then you switch on the trembler coil, there's a subdued hum from the little mahogany coil box on the dash and the engine bursts into life. If this doesn't work, then you have to crank the engine.

With the engine running, you depress the clutch pedal – almost certainly it's a cone clutch – and engage first gear.

The steering wheel, surprisingly small, with a thick mahogany rim, carries at its centre the ignition and throttle levers. You adjust the ignition to give maximum power without pinking, and put your foot down.

The engine – most likely a four-cylinder side valve T- or L-head unit – is hardly turbine-smooth, for the fashionably long stroke isn't conducive to mechanical quietness. You're conscious of the whir of the timing gears and the rattle of the tappets: the updraught carburetter hisses with the intake of air, and there's a medley of lesser sounds.

Typical Edwardian giant – the 8-litre 42/70-h.p. Bianchi, 1913, an obvious copy of contemporary Mercedes practice

The engine, rigidly bolted to the chassis sidemembers or mounted in a girder subframe, sends vibrations up through the soles of your feet and the palms of your hands. A slight movement of the wheel will suffice to turn quite an acute corner, for the steering ratio is almost direct, yet it's not too heavy, for the big wheels with their high-pressure tyres roll easily over the rough road surface: and unhindered by brakes, the front wheels have a surprisingly sharp lock.

99

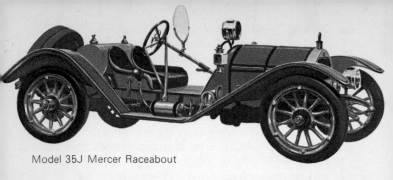

Model 35J Mercer Raceabout

Once the car is moving at the correct speed, you can lift your foot; the heavy flywheel will keep the motor turning steadily on a whiff of throttle. The rear axle is geared high, so the revolutions are low, and provided you keep the car's momentum up, surprisingly high cross-country averages can be maintained.

The development of the sporting car was rapid. A notable step forward took place in 1911, when a Rolls-Royce endowed with torpedo coachwork of surpassing beauty – a most unusual thing for 1911 – ran from London to Edinburgh using only its 2·9:1 top gear ratio, covering 24·32 miles per gallon, and then achieved 78·26 m.p.h. at Brooklands, knocking a previous ''top-gear'' run by a 65-h.p. Napier into a cocked hat.

The London-Edinburgh Rolls was not the first Rolls-Royce sporting car, but it was the first to appear since C. S. Rolls had

been killed the previous summer when his Wright Flyer crashed at the Bournemouth Aviation Meeting. It was really a Grand Tourer rather than an out-and-out sports car, for none of the traditional Rolls-Royce virtues of silence and smoothness of running were abandoned, and the speed capabilities of the car were due rather to efficient body design than engine performance – a maximum power output of some 50 b.h.p. at 1,700 r.p.m. was hardly remarkable for 7·4 litres, even then.

Limited production of the type, one of the most handsome cars of the period, was undertaken, and James Radley, a pioneer aviator, entered a modified "Continental" version in the Austrian Alpine Tour of 1912, the event which had taken the place of the Prince Henry Trial in the sporting calendar. The Katschberg Pass proved too much for the high bottom gear of the Rolls' three-speed box, and Radley was disqualified for dropping two passengers to make the ascent.

The "Continental" model was fitted with four forward gears after that, and a team of four swept the board in the 1913 Alpine, while Radley's car *"Alpine Eagle"* won the City of Trieste prize in the 1914 event.

Compared to the Rolls-Royce, the American sporting car of the period was crude and unrefined – but its performance was rather more exciting. The *beau ideal* of American sporting cars was incontestably the 4·9-litre Mercer Type 35 Raceabout, designed by Finlay Robertson Porter and guaranteed to cover a mile in 51 seconds.

London-Edinburgh Rolls-Royce

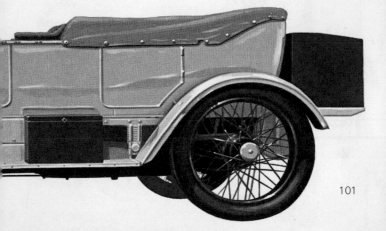

Technical Advances

It is fairly safe to say that virtually every major design feature of the modern car was pioneered before the Great War. In 1914, for example, Louis Renault proposed a "Hydrolastic" suspension, although he probably never built it , and the 1904 20-h.p. Hutton had hydraulic brakes and a complex automatic transmission. What was lacking in those days was the ability to make these advanced features cheap and durable, and of course, the right materials were either unavailable or prohibitively expensive.

The sensation of the Paris Show in 1903 was a 50-h.p. racing car produced by the previously unremarkable Dutch firm of Spyker. This machine had a six-cylinder engine – one of the first cars with this feature – four-wheel-drive and brakes acting on all four wheels. For a while it was almost invincible at hillclimbs, and the company even produced some touring cars driven on all wheels: but by 1906 they had returned to conventionality.

In 1906 the Adams Manufacturing Co, of Bedford, marketed a remarkable 60-h.p. car, with a V-8 engine closely patterned on the Antoinette aero-engine designed by the Frenchman Levavasseur, for which they held the British production rights. They also built a V-16 Antoinette engine, but this does not seem to have been used in a car. Adams were also noted for

Riding on air – the 1913 Cowey light car

Antoinette-powered: the Adams V8

their "Pedals to Push, That's All" epicyclic transmission, in which a row of pedals engaged the gears.

Like all conventional epicyclic gears, the Adams transmission suffered from excessive wear at the hands of the unskilled drivers for whom it was intended, and a sliding gearbox became available as an option (or a replacement).

Independent front suspension is, as has been mentioned elsewhere, virtually as old as the motor vehicle, but a suspension system which did not receive the publicity it merited was fitted to the 1913 Cowey light car; its Chapuis-Dornier engine also worked a pump which supplied compressed air through pipes to pneumatic suspension units at each corner of the chassis. Though apparently simple in operation, the Cowey suspension just didn't catch on.

The rich American inventor Walter Christie was an indefatigable supporter of front wheel drive. He built tourers and taxis incorporating this feature, and fearsome racers with transverse V-4 engines and direct drive from the end of the

crankshaft. He even entered one for the 1907 French Grand Prix, where its racing number "WC-1" caused vast amusement, as did the frequency with which it broke down. Somehow Christie's cars were not as much of a success as he made out, and lacked the basic ability to proceed in a straight line.

Another man with a fixity of purpose was Harry Ferguson, Belfast motor agent and pioneer aviator. With his brothers he helped to design a "People's Car" known as the Fergus, which cut maintenance to a minimum. A few points had to be checked or topped up every six months, instead of the myriad greasers on the average car which needed attention at least once a week. Unfortunately, the car was introduced in 1915, and, although limited production was undertaken in New Jersey after the war, the car never really had a chance. It did, however, give Harry Ferguson the idea for a car which could go where there were no roads in the accepted sense of the word, and led him into experiments with four-wheel-drive.

The 1915 Fergus

Whereas it was easy enough to make cars go fast the real problem was how to stop them. From 1904, manufacturers became interested in producing fourwheel braking systems. In 1906 Mercedes experimented with external contracting brakes actuated by cables, but the effect of such fitments on the suspension and axles of the day was feared by motorists, not without justification. In 1910 Isotta-Fraschini standardised front-wheel brakes on certain of their models, and the next year the Scottish firm of Argyll followed suit. But it was to be 15 years before brakes on all four wheels became universal.

One should not forget, either, that bicycles fitted with crude hydraulic brakes were on show at the 1895 National Cycle Exhibition, or that in 1893 tubeless low-pressure balloon tyres on disc wheels of small diameter were first introduced.

Mercedes front-wheel brake, 1906

Cars at War

A Locomobile steam car and a fleet of steam lorries had been used with some success in the Boer War, and the British Army carried out trials of motor lorries in 1901 and set up motorised units in the years prior to 1914. In 1911 they inaugurated a subsidy scheme by which the owners of petrol lorries conforming to War Office specifications were paid an annual sum on condition that their vehicles were kept in good order and were immediately available for army service. The result was that when war broke out, some 1,200 lorries were ready to supply the British Expeditionary Force during the Battle of Mons.

After Von Kluck's attack on Paris in September 1914 was foiled by General Gallieni commandeering the city's taxis to rush 6,000 French reinforcements to a weak point on the German flank at night (the cab company received the full fare shown on the meters, plus a 27% tip for the driver, too!), it was generally agreed that the internal combustion engine would play a major role in the hostilities.

Just as important was the use of a fleet of London buses to move British infantry rapidly to the front: at least 1,300 of the

Royal Flying Corps Crossley tender

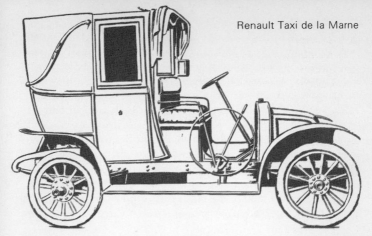

LGOC's B-types served in Belgium and Flanders. The Royal Naval Air Service converted two into armoured cars during the opening months of the war, and the Belgian Army fought alongside them in armoured Minerva luxury cars. Later in the war, armoured Rolls-Royces and Lanchesters were to serve with the British Army.

Prewar experiments with caterpillar-tracked vehicles by the Lincoln firm of Ruston & Hornsby proved invaluable when the tank was under development. The prototype tank, "Willie", was completed in December 1915, by William Foster & Co.; it could reach the terrifying speed of $3\frac{1}{2}$ m.p.h.

In August 1916, the tank was a fighting proposition, and 50 were sent to France under conditions of great secrecy, where they went into action on the Somme on September 15. Tanks were a most effective weapon, and won many notable victories, notably Cambrai (November 1917) and Amiens (August 1918).

The motor vehicle, in fact, took over all sectors of military transport: the French used Bébé Peugeots for dispatch riding, and had a penchant for converting old racing cars into high speed staff transport; dependent on their rank, British officers rode in Rolls-Royce, Vauxhall or Sunbeam staff cars (though the Royal Flying Corps favoured the Crossley), and German officers favoured a wide range of cars, from the 21-litre 200-h.p. Benz, through such rarities as Stoewer and Komnick down to the crazy front-wheel-driven 10-h.p. Phanomobil.

Cars for the Masses

War service instilled a sense of the utility of the motor car into vast numbers of servicemen who had not previously shown any interest in owning one: once they were demobilised they could hardly wait to spend their meagre service gratuity on a car of their own. Both in Britain and France a whole new motor industry mushroomed, mostly made up of a couple of enthusiasts working in a back-street workshop on limited capital, with limited means, or firms which had suddenly found themselves with factories full of workers and expensive machinery but no work because of the Armistice and turned to making cars, motorcycles, saucepans or furniture to try and stay in business.

One of the few men in the latter class who really went about motor manufacture properly was André Citroën, who had

Citroën *Trèfle,* 1922

studied American methods of mass-production at first hand. Taking a leaf from Henry Ford's book, he began producing a single model in his factory at the Quai de Javel, Paris, a fully-equipped 10-h.p. torpedo made in such large numbers that it could be sold at a very low price. By 1922, 100 Citroëns a day were leaving the works. The new 1·4-litre 5-cv. model, designed by Jules Salomon, had three-seat "cloverleaf" coachwork in a distinctive shade of yellow which earned the car the punning nickname *"Citron pressé"* (lemonade). It was produced officially under licence in Milan, and unofficially in Germany as the Opel "Laubfrosch". Some 65,000 5-cv.s were made in France before production ceased in May 1926,

Peugeot Quadrilette, 1924

and both this and the Opel version dominated their respective national markets and caused the demise of many smaller firms, even though the cars built by the latter may have been cheaper.

The little Citroen 5-cv. was relatively large when compared with its contemporary rival, the Peugeot Quadrilette. This was really a super-cyclecar, with a minuscule 667-c.c. engine, the smallest four-cylinder unit then built. The track was so narrow that the two seats were either set in tandem or staggered (although side-by-side seating for very good friends was provided in cars destined for England), and if the back wheels had been 30 inches closer, it would have been a three-wheeler.

It was with this car in mind that Sir Herbert Austin closeted himself in the billiard room at his home and began to plan a tiny four-seater car which would appeal to the family man who could only afford the price of a motorcycle and sidecar.

Despite opposition from his colleagues, Austin put the Austin Seven on the market in 1922, and had a runaway success, for it outsold all Austin's other models put together.

The "experts" took it seriously too, when E. C. Gordon England began beating 1,100-c.c. cars in a racing Seven at Brooklands at lap speeds of over 75 m.p.h.

W. R. Morris was a cycle and motor agent in Oxford who in 1913 had started production of a high quality light car known as the Morris-Oxford, with a 1,018-c.c. engine. By 1914, 100 were being turned out a month, quite a high figure for those

Sporting-bodied
1916 Morris Cowley

days, but the chassis could only accommodate two-seater coachwork (and it was a tight squeeze at that, for Morris had designed the bodywork round his own slight proportions). He planned a larger-engined four-seater version, but found that the cost would be greatly increased. In 1913, he went to America to see how they managed to build down to a price, and ended by ordering most of the components including the engines, 1,495-c.c. Continental "Red Seal" units, in the U.S.

In 1915 the first Morris-Cowley four-seater appeared, at the extremely competitive price of £165 18s, its American origins betrayed by the central gear lever. A few hundred Cowleys were produced during the war, but then the imposition of the McKenna import duties made the use of American components uneconomic, so Morris acquired the rights to the "Red Seal" design, and had his engines built in Coventry by the English branch of Hotchkiss, French armament manufacturers.

The post-war boom fizzled out in 1920, and sales of all makes slowed down considerably. Drastic price cuts, paring profit to the bone, were made by the Bean Car Co. in late 1920 but without much result.

Morris, with a factory full of unsold cars, followed this example (and perhaps that of Henry Ford) in February 1921, cutting the prices of his cars by up to £100. He had chosen the right time, for sales almost doubled, 3,077 cars being built in 1921 against 1,932 in 1920, and the "Bullnose" Morris soon became Britain's best-selling car. Morris acquired all his component suppliers, so that he could gear up production by having enough of the right parts in the right place at the right time, and as a result output doubled and trebled so that in 1925, 54,151 Morrises were made, at a basic price of £175 (but the Ford-type moving assembly line didn't come until the 1930s).

In 1922 the Wolverhampton firm of Clyno introduced a 1,386-c.c. car to compete with the Bullnose. In many ways the Clyno was the better car: its steering was based on that of a Grand Prix Peugeot owned by one of its sponsors; it was earlier in the field with four-wheel brakes; it was faster, and its gearbox (with righthand change from 1924) was quieter (the second gear of the Bullnose was renowned for emitting a tram-like shriek, audible long before the car came into sight). Clyno always offered their cars at exactly the same price as Morris, and by 1926 were the third largest manufacturers in the country, turning out 300 cars a week from an improbably small factory.

The ill-considered introduction of a "£100" 9-h.p. model and the construction of a vast new factory caused their demise in early 1929. It was so unnecessary, for they needn't have tried so hard to beat Morris. Their expensive "Royal" model sold ten times better than their economy line.

The author's 1927 Clyno
10·8 h.p. Royal tourer

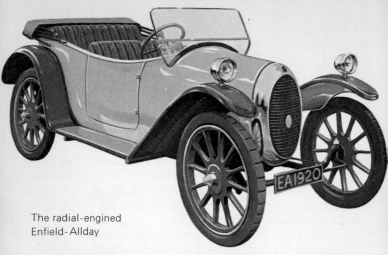

The radial-engined
Enfield-Allday

During the Great War, many British motor manufacturers built aero-engines or their components: but it is surprising how little effect this had on their post-Armistice productions. Clyno for example, made ABC Dragonfly radials, but their cars, though quite speedy, used bought-out Coventry-Climax sidevalve engines, while Austin, who built some 2,500 aero-engines of all types, from small rotaries to a V-12 250-h.p. unit, produced only lethargic sidevalve cars whose potential performance was nullified by inept manifolding. Where aero-engineering principles *were* applied to cars, the results could be most interesting, although the negligible performance of the single overhead camshaft Wolseleys of the early 1920s suggests that their wartime experience in building Hispano-Suiza aeroengines had not been put to the best possible use.

The most striking ''aircraft-influenced'' car of the period (if one excludes the crazy French Marcel Leyat, which had a British-built ABC *Scorpion* flat-twin aero-engine in its nose driving an airscrew, and steered with its centre-pivoted *rear* axle) was the Enfield-Allday, which had a 1,453-c.c. five-cylinder radial air-cooled engine with pushrod operated concentric annular valves in the detachable cylinder heads, developed 23 b.h.p. and weighed only 123 lb. The chassis, mounted on cantilever springs all round, was formed of two triangulated pressed-steel girders set about a foot apart, the apices being mounted uppermost with the gearbox slung on trunnions between them. The body was carried on outriggers from this frame, and was notably low-slung for the period.

The Enfield-Allday was the sensation of the 1919 Olympia Show, but all those innovations were too much to manufacture at an economical price, and perhaps half-a-dozen (definitely four) were built before the company turned to a more conventional design. Almost as unorthodox was the three-cylinder radial engined CAR of 1920, with coil-spring suspension, designed by Roy Fedden of Straker-Squire. It too, succumbed to financial pressures.

More typical of the aircooled light cars of the post war era was the 998-c.c. flat-twin Rover 8 of 1920-24, of which some 10,000 were sold in the first two years of production. A wide range of bodies was available, although the price range was (in 1922) from £180 to £240. Despite the maker's claim that "the painting and upholstery are worthy of the car, which we try to turn out so well finished that owners are encouraged to

Flat-twin Rover 8

take an interest in keeping their cars smart," the Rover 8 had an undeniably "clockwork mouse" appearance which was not dispelled by the characteristic whir of its engine.

As in Britain, there was an upsurge of demand for new cars in America following the cessation of hostilities. Henry Ford had already shown that the car of the future was the cheap mass-produced unit, and although his lead in this field appeared incontestable, nevertheless he had some serious rivals, notably Overland and General Motors.

Overland, controlled by John North Willys, was America's second best selling car, in a slightly higher price bracket than Ford, while General Motors had originally been formed in 1908 by William Crapo Durant as a combine of small and medium-sized companies – Buick, Oldsmobile, Cadillac and Oakland among them. The list would have included Ford, but Henry Ford demanded $3 million in cash, which Durant couldn't raise. By 1910, General Motors had run out of money, and were only salvaged by a takeover by a banking syndicate, which not unnaturally fired Billy Durant.

Undeterred, he joined forces in 1911 with racing driver Louis Chevrolet to produce cars to the latter's designs: but Durant wanted to build a Ford-beater, not the beautifully engineered cars planned by Chevrolet, who left the company in 1913. The early Chevrolets, especially the "490" (so-called because of its planned price) sold well, and by 1916 Durant was able to exchange enough Chevrolet shares for General Motors shares to regain control.

A popular American six-cylinder model: the 1929 Essex Super Six

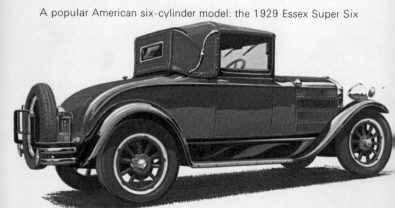

Model A Ford, as modified during the Spanish Civil War

The post-war boom in sales was followed rapidly by a decline. The biggest companies, heavily over-extended by development programmes, were hardest hit. Henry Ford, who had just spent $100 million in buying out his stockholders, was constructing a $116 milion factory at Dearborn, owed $8 million in back dividends, and had a $75 million bank loan falling due in 1921. In September 1920, the slump had brought new car sales to a virtual standstill, so Ford slashed the price of the Model T from $575 to $440 to get things moving again, and compelled his dealers to pay cash for their consignments of cars, or lose their lucrative franchises – this solved *his* problems. At the same time, Billy Durant had heavily over-committed his personal resources to the tune of some $30 million, and was ousted from GM by his backer Pierre Du Pont. His replacement, Alfred P. Sloan, guided the fortunes of Chevrolet so ably that in 1927 it became America's best-selling car, a lead which Ford could not regain.

That year Henry Ford had at last been persuaded that the Model T was completely outdated, and had halted production after 15,007,003 had been built. Even though its price had reached an all-time low of $290, sales were dropping off.

After a six-month hiatus, the Model A was introduced to replace it. Those who had expected a vehicle as non-conformist as the T were disappointed by the A's utter conventionality.

Aero-engined Monsters

In Britain after the Armistice it was both easy and cheap to acquire brand new aero-engines from the Aircraft Disposals Board, and impecunious enthusiasts found that by fitting such an engine in an elderly chassis from some large pre-war car, a fast racer could be constructed which stood every chance of success at Brooklands.

The first, and most successful, aero-engined racer was, however, a rather more considered project, designed by Louis Coatalen of Sunbeam round an 18·3 litre V-12 Sunbeam *Manitou* engine, as used in wartime naval aeroplanes. The single-seat body and channel-steel chassis were specially built for this car, which first appeared in the autumn of 1920. It had many racing successes, and also broke the world speed record three times: in 1922 driven by Kenelm Lee Guinness, (133·75 m.p.h.) – this was the last occasion that this record was broken on a closed racing circuit; in 1924, Malcolm Campbell (146·16 m.p.h.) and 1925 (Campbell again, 150·87 m.p.h.).

In quite a different category was the celebrated *Chitty-Chitty-Bang-Bang* (its onomatopoeic name came from a ribald wartime song), owned by Count Louis Vorow Zborowski.

Chitty-Chitty-Bang-Bang I, as owned by Adrian Conan Doyle in the late 1920s

This chain-driven monster was formed by dropping a 23-litre Maybach engine into a 75-h.p. Mercedes chassis, and endowing the result with coachwork of exceptional crudity. It first raced at Brooklands at Easter 1921, and showed that despite its uncouth appearance it could motor surprisingly effectively by winning its first race from the V-12 Sunbeam at 100·75 m.p.h. *Chitty* seems to have been somewhat of a handful, and in 1922 was badly damaged when it left the track as the result of a burst tyre, and although rebuilt, never seemed to regain its former zest. Zborowski built a further two *Chitties,* of which one still exists, and then the largest car to run at Brooklands, the *Higham Special*, with a 27-litre V-12 Liberty engine.

An 11½-litre V-12 Wolseley *Viper* aeroengine was fitted into an old Napier chassis by the larger-than-life Competition Manager of Wolseley, Captain Alastair Miller, Bart., and, although desperately nose-heavy, scored some successes driven by the then relatively unknown Kaye Don.

Ernest Eldridge, one of the cleverest British racing car designers of the 1920s, converted his 1907 Isotta-Fraschini chassis to take a 20½-litre Maybach engine, and followed this up by installing a 21·7-litre Fiat aviation motor in the chassis of the famous FIAT *Mephistopheles,* after unwise tuning by John Duff had blown up the original power unit.

The 'Car Superexcellent' — the 30/98 Vauxhall

The Vintage Sports Car

Most 1919 British sports cars were based on 1914 designs, so a great deal of interest was aroused when it was learned that W. O. Bentley planned to produce an entirely new 3-litre machine capable of touring speeds of 60 m.p.h. or more over any road surface. Bentley and his design team began work in January 1919; the first car was complete enough to exhibit at the Motor Show that year, and was tested by S. C. H. Davis of *The Autocar* in December 1919. For a number of reasons, financial and technical, production didn't get under way until September 1921.

The Bentley wasn't cheap by any standards. All bought-out components were specially manufactured to Bentley's requirements, and the 1923 price of £1,395 for the standard touring model was astronomical: no other vehicle in the popular 15·9-h.p. taxation class came within £500 of it, and you could buy four 16/20 Cubitts (backed by S. F. Edge) and have £10 left over from the same amount. But the 80 b.h.p. output of one Bentley was almost as much as the combined efforts of four Cubitts, the car was guaranteed to reach 80 m.p.h. on Brooklands – and its close-ratio gearbox was designed with acceleration in mind.

Had it got into full production, I think that the six-cylinder o.h.c. 3·9-litre 24/90-h.p. Straker-Squire (1923 price £1,450 complete) would have been a serious contender for the Bentley's market, as its engine, based on the Rolls-Royce Eagle aviation motor, was also capable of developing 80 b.h.p.: and the all-up weight was a couple of hundredweights less.

As it was, the only other serious choice in the British fast tourer field in the immediate post-Armistice period was one of those re-hashed pre-war designs, the 30/98 Vauxhall, derived by L. H. Pomeroy from the Prince Henry type in 1914. But what a car! The fluted radiator and bonnet, for so long the "trademark" of Vauxhall, usually fronted elegant *Velox* fourseater coachwork, but in 1924 the supremely elegant *Wensum* body also became available.

The 4½-litre side-valve engine of the E-type 30/98 put out some 100 b.h.p.: about 270 E-types were made before the model was supplanted by the 4·2 litre OE-type with pushrod ohv, developing 112 b.h.p. – about 310 of these were built before the 30/98 succumbed in 1927 to the General Motors takeover of Vauxhall.

At £1,300, the "Car Superexcellent" was a rather better buy than a Bentley: 30/98s were still racing successfully at Brooklands in the early 1930s, proving to the full Vauxhall's 1921

With many Brooklands successes to its credit, this special-bodied 3-litre Bentley once belonged to Woolf Barnato

claim: "the finest of sporting cars . . . it will last for years and cost very little for wear-and-tear repairs."

One of the more delightful features of the vintage era of motoring was the way in which tiny firms teetering on the brink of insolvency could produce better sports cars than the giants of the industry: and each marque had its own little *coterie* of enthusiasts. But none were more dedicated than the handful who bought what *The Automotor Journal* referred to as "a world-beating car built in Kensington with a hacksaw and a file" – the Aston Martin.

In 1919, the prototype Aston Martin, on which work had begun in 1914, was the first car to climb the notorious 1 in $2\frac{1}{2}$ gradient of Alms Hill near Henley-on-Thames, without stopping, and a few months later, Lionel Martin drove another Aston Martin to victory in one of the first post-American race meetings at Brooklands. At £695, the side-valve Aston Martin was virtually the most expensive $1\frac{1}{2}$-litre car on the market – it was even dearer than the 16-valve o.h.c. "Modified Brescia" Bugatti.

Two cars were built for Clive Gallop and Count Zborowski (who financed the company) to drive in the 1922 Grand Prix with Henry-inspired 16-valve twin o.h.c. engines: the first two of these power units were built by Rover, who omitted the thrust bearing from the crankshaft and the resultant stresses broke off the end of the front main bearing.

Aston Martin's first competition car, the 1921 sidevalve *Bunny*, was far more successful. Racing honours could not conceal the company's inadequate finances, however, and soon after Zborowski's death at Monza in 1924 they went into liquidation, having produced perhaps 60 cars; the name was later revived.

'Duck's-back' 12/50 Alvis

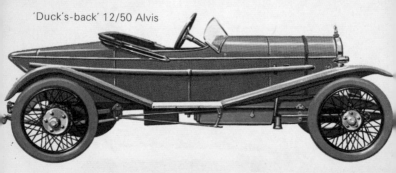

1930/7 TT Replica Frazer Nash

Better fortune attended the Coventry firm of Alvis, who began building side-valve 10/30 h.p. cars in 1920: in 1923 came an overhead valve 10/30 Super-sports model with pointed "duck's back" polished aluminium coachwork, which was soon boosted in capacity to become the 12/50, one of the best-loved of all vintage sports cars. The success of this model enabled Alvis to survive a prolonged and severe financial crisis: each week seven cars had to be sold by Henly's, the London agents, before the wages could be paid at Coventry.

When the GN cyclecar began to develop into a light car of

1930 M-Type
M.G. Midget

122

less than usual interest, its designers, H. R. Godfrey and Archie Frazer-Nash, left the company to begin production of a sports car using the old-type GN gearchange by chain dog-clutches. The stark and lively Frazer Nash car was produced in almost unchanged form from 1925 to 1938 (about 350 were built), and had the elegance of line of a true thoroughbred.

Although the archetypal car of the 1920s was the staid family tourer, it took little more than mild tuning of the engine (more often than not a proprietary sidevalve unit) and the fitting of light coachwork to turn such a workhorse into a fairly nippy sports car. One of the best examples of this metamorphosis was the MG, the brainchild of Cecil Kimber, general manager of the Morris Garages, Oxford, a wholly-owned subsidiary of Morris Motors devoted to the sales and servicing of, and the fitting of, special coachwork to, Morris cars.

In February 1923, Kimber modified an 11·9 h.p. Morris-Cowley for competition work, and won a gold medal in the London-Land's End Trial. Having discovered the performance

1929 MG 18/80 Salonette

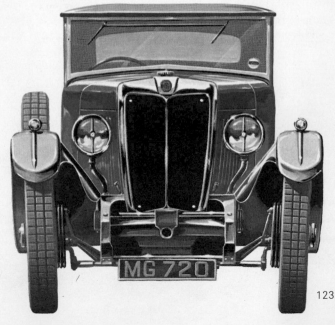

potential of the Morris engine, Kimber built a handful of 11·9 h.p. Morris Cowley Specials, with rakish two-seater bodies with a single dickey seat in the tapered tail. The first of these cars was sold for £300 in June 1923.

In March 1924 Kimber introduced the Morris-Oxford based 14/28 MG, as the products of the Morris Garages were henceforth to be known. About this time he built for his own use an o.h.v. Hotchkiss-engined trials car with a Morris chassis often erroneously referred to as "MG No. 1" which had virtually no influence at all on the development of the MG. By 1928, the 14/28 had become the 14/40 Mk IV, and a new £16,000 factory at Edmund Road, Cowley, had been set up.

A significant step forward in the MG story took place in 1927, when Sir William Morris acquired the ailing Wolseley company, and with it the Hispano-Suiza-inspired overhead camshaft engine design. Two new Morrises using versions of this were unveiled at the 1928 Motor Show: the 2·5-litre "Six" and the 847 c.c. Minor. At the same show, MG unveiled their new 18/80 six-cylinder model and the diminutive pointed-tail fabric two-seater Midget. Although these cars were obviously sisters under the skin to the new Morrises, their performance was in quite a different category. The Midget, especially, captured the public imagination, for it could better 65 m.p.h. and 40 m.p.g., yet cost only £175.

CGS Grand Sport Amilcar

Soon the little cars were making their mark in competition, which served to show up some dire deficiences in the standard Morris camshaft timing – this was rectified on 1930 models.

France, too, had a considerable "back-street motor industry". It has been stated that there were 350 firms producing cars there in 1920, 80 per cent of them based in Paris.

Most of these tiny companies specialised in stark sports cars, for the impecunious sporting motorist didn't incline to be fussy over matters of comfort, finish or noise – and anyway who could hope to compete with Renault, Citroën or Peugeot? Ironically, these three are the only companies to survive today out of the 350. Most of the noisy voiturettes quickly vanished into well-deserved limbo, but a select few proved themselves capable of better things. Among these were the BNC (Bollack, Netter & Cie) and its cousin the Lombard, the Benjamin and the Sénéchal. But above all there were the Amilcar and its great rival the Salmson.

The Amilcar first saw the light of day in 1920, the product of a company formed by two engineers from the ailing Le Zèbre company, Morel and Moyet, and two financiers, Emil Akar and Joseph Lamy, from whose names was concocted the word "Amilcar". The original Amilcar, the type CC, was intended as an economical runabout, but its performance, due to an all-up weight of $8\frac{1}{2}$ cwt., was exceptionally lively and soon a sports version appeared.

In 1922, Morel won the first 24-hour *Bol d'Or*, but the real *forte* of the side-valve Amilcars was hill-climbing. With its two staggered seats, pointed tail and rakish mudwings, the Amilcar, especially in its Grand Sport CGS and Surbaissé GGSs forms, sold in great numbers – between 1926 and 1928 35 Amilcars were produced daily at the company's St Denis factory. Also catalogued were potent Cozette-supercharged twin o.h.c. six-cylinder racing cars – under the sponsorship of Vernon Balls, the British agent, these monopolised the 1,100 c.c. class in the annual Junior Car Club 200-Mile Race at Brooklands in 1926-27-28.

The beginnings of the Salmson seemed inauspicious enough, for the company, which had constructed aeroengines at its Billancourt factory during the war, acquired a licence to build British GN cyclecars. However, they soon got over this,

and began producing sporting voiturettes with never a trace of cyclecar about them. Originally, their cars had an odd overhead valve gear, in which the inlet and exhaust valves of each cylinder were operated by the same "push-and-pull-rod". Later, twin overhead camshafts were standardised, although cheaper Salmsons still had twin bearing cranks.

The sports car, in the European sense, hardly existed in America. The 1915-designed L-head 22/70 h.p. Mercer, successor to the celebrated "Raceabout" just about lasted into the 1920s, but it was very much on its own. To the average rich American owner, a sporting car was a second car, an elegant means of arriving at the golf club or yacht basin. Its flowing lines, owing more to artistic styling than aerodynamics, and often picked out in bizarre colour schemes, were designed for the carriage sweeps of West Egg, not the race track. It was usually built on a standard "quality" chassis, such as Packard, Pierce-Arrow or Jordan (Ned Jordan was renowned for his flamboyant advertising prose: but the car, described as "the cross of the wild and the tame", leaned heavily towards the latter).

In 1927 Stutz cars were entered for all bar one of the races organised by the Automobile Association of America: they won every one. Famous racing driver Frank Lockhart designed America's first boat-tail speedster body for the Stutz in 1927. This handsome car (Stutz used worm drive to lower the centre of gravity) was good for over 105 m.p.h. with a 3·8:1 final drive ratio.

The handsomest of the breed was the six-cylinder 4·7-litre Kissel Custom-built Speedster which appeared in 1919, directly developed from the Kissel Kar Silver Special Speedster of 1917, and named "Gold Bug" as the result of a contest for a $5 prize held in the *Milwaukee Journal,* whose Automobile Editor, W. W. "Brownie" Rowland, owned one of the earliest of the type. Distinctive features of the Kissel Gold Bug were a golf-bag holder on the rear wing and extra seats which pulled out from either side of the body above the running board. The Gold Bug was succeeded in the mid-1920s by the eight-cylinder White Eagle 126, a handsome car by any standards.

The nearest approach the U.S. made to producing a European-style sports car was in 1926, when the Stutz Motor Car Co introduced their new "vertical eight" 4·7-litre model, one of the outstanding American cars of the 1920s. A single chain-driven overhead camshaft acted directly on the 16 valves, and the engine was designed and built to eliminate vibration entirely. There were nine main bearings, of $2\frac{1}{2}$ in. diameter, and full pressurised oil feed was standard. The construction of the chassis was exceptionally rigid, and hydraulic fourwheel brakes were fitted.

At the end of the vintage period, Stutz introduced an even more fabulous machine, the twin o.h.c., 16-valve DV 32.

32-h.p. straight-eight Minerva

Cars for the Rich

The aeroengine of the Great War was unquestionably the 150 h.p. V-8 o.h.c. Hispano-Suiza: it powered the famous Spad 7, standard equipment for the French *escadrilles de chasse,* and the SE5, Britain's finest fighting scout, was designed round the "Hisso", which was built in Britain as the Wolseley Viper. This power unit was designed by Marc Birkigt, a talented Swiss engineer who had gone to Barcelona in 1899 aged 21 and had later joined the Castro car company, which by 1904 was going down for the third time in very deep financial waters. The company was reconstituted, Birkigt was made factory manager, and the firm became, elegantly but ungrammatically, *La Hispano-Suiza.* Their earliest products were unremarkable 3·8 and 2·2 litre fours, but in 1910 came the famous "Alfonso XIII" sporting model. Nothing that had gone before, however, gave any indication as to the form of the post-war Hispano-Suiza (it should have been Franco-Hispano-Suiza now, for another factory had been set up at Bois-Colombes, near Paris, shortly before the war).

Birkigt had drawn heavily on his aeroengine experience, and had produced a magnificent 6·6-litre six-cylinder power unit developing 135 b.h.p., with a single overhead camshaft and a light-alloy cylinder block with screwed-in steel liners. This was mounted in a rigid chassis of equally advanced design, which featured servo-assisted fourwheel braking: but the gearbox had three widely spaced (and noisy) ratios, and was obviously not intended for rapid acceleration.

Great car, noisy gearbox:
37-h.p. Hispano-Suiza

Owners praised the impeccable road-manners of the Hispano, which could be had in Britain at a price of around £2,600 in 1923 with a body by one of the leading Paris *carossiers*. This was about the same as a Rolls-Royce Ghost, and the Hispano was incontestably the better bargain: perhaps the only car more desirable than the 6·6-litre Hispano was the mighty 8-litre "Boulogne" introduced alongside it in 1923.

Less costly, but equally as elegant was the straight-eight Isotta-Fraschini from Milan, introduced in 6-litre form in 1918, and enlarged to 7·3-litres in 1925: but its handling was nowhere near the standard set by the Hispano.

Belgium's contribution to the luxury car stakes was the Minerva, available after the war in 3·6-litre four- and 5·4-litre six-cylinder form. The latter continued in production until 1927, when it was supplanted by the 6-litre 32-34 h.p., which had a 12½-foot wheelbase. The clientele that Minerva was aiming for is summed up in the following passage from their

Great car, heavy steering: straight-eight Isotta-Fraschini

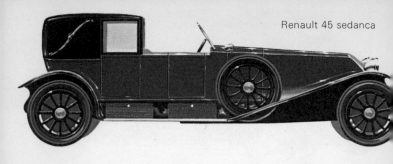

1920 handbook: "On the rear portion of cardan tube casing there is arranged a small plug which should be unscrewed every 2,000 miles and a wine-glassful of oil poured in".

The type of owner who purchased elegance by the yard could do no better than to buy a 45 h.p. Renault, which devoted almost half of its overall length of more than 16 feet to keeping its monstrous 9·1-litre six-cylinder engine dry. This was the largest car to be produced in Europe in the 1920s on a serious basis – although Daimler made a handful of their 1912-designed 9·5 litre 57 h.p. cars in 1924 at the behest of George V, who shared his father's liking for this ugly breed – and it was a car capable of an exceptional performance: a streamlined 45 h.p. saloon broke the 24-hour record in July 1926 at an average of 106·5 m.p.h. The "baby" 7·1-litre *Reinastella* which succeeded it in 1929 had nothing like the same *panache*.

Under their new Chief Engineer, L.H. Pomeroy, Daimler attempted to dispel their "funeral-carriage" image by bringing out in 1926 a 7·1-litre "Double-Six" V-12 which retained such antique features as a push-on handbrake and a five-spoke steering-wheel; but the servicing and cold-weather-starting

Rolls-Royce Phantom I sedanca

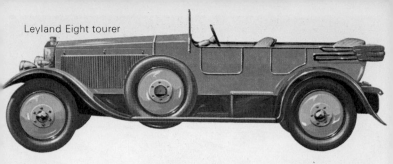

Leyland Eight tourer

problems associated with a 12-cylinder double-sleeve-valve engine of horrendous complexity hardly bear thinking about.

No wonder many people played safe and bought Rolls-Royce Ghosts, even though the design was desperately out-moded in the mid-1920s: the 3·1-litre Twenty introduced by Rolls in 1922 displayed much American influence, which displeased the traditionalists. Its pushrod o.h.v. engine paved the way for the Phantom of 1925 which replaced the Ghost, but retained its Edwardian chassis. Rolls-Royce decided against using their hard-earned experience in overhead camshaft aero-engine design in the new engine, which was a pity, although Napier's 1920 o.h.c. 40/50 had shown the folly of allying a modern engine to an antique chassis.

George Lanchester certainly had no fear of the overhead camshaft: the 6·2-litre 40 h.p. Lanchester straight-8 of 1919-1928 was so equipped and it was a very refined thoroughbred indeed, quite unlike the uncouth machines which bore the name after Daimler took the company over in 1930.

Just as advanced was the V-8 4-litre Guy of 1919 with auto-matic chassis lubrication which was made in small numbers by the Wolverhampton commercial vehicle firm. Sidney Guy had worked for Sunbeam, and it is quite likely that there was a good deal of Coatalen influence in the design of the V-8's power unit.

Another firm of lorry builders who briefly essayed luxury car production was Leyland Motors, of Lancashire, whose Parry Thomas-designed 7,266 c.c. Eight (the original cars were of 6,967 c.c.) was the sensation of the 1920 Olympia Show. Intended as "the most perfect car it is possible to design and manufacture", the Leyland Eight sold at a chassis price of

Abner Doble's personal Doble Steamer

£2,500 (later reduced to £1,875). Lubrication was fully automatic, and everywhere the chassis, with torsion-bar-aided rear suspension, bore evidence of Thomas' genius.

Nowhere in the world was the high-priced luxury car more appreciated than in America. Imported cars had a snobbish cachet all their own, as Rolls-Royce found to their cost when they set up a manufacturing subsidiary in Springfield, Massachusetts, only to find that the wealthy *preferred* to pay more for an imported Rolls. Much of this snobbery, I think, stemmed from the inability of the average American coachbuilder to create truly elegant bodies: their products had either the plebeian air of the production line or else were spoiled by a Christmas-tree proliferation of irrelevant decoration and ugly accessories. Thus some quite remarkable vehicles have never received the attention they deserve in Europe.

The Model A Duesenberg of 1920-28 was one such. The Duesenberg brothers, Fred and August, had learned many useful lessons from their brief wartime experience in producing the unsuccessful 16-cylinder Bugatti aeroengine (two straight-eights mounted side by side on a common crankcase, with the crankshafts geared together). The 4·3-litre straight-eight Duesenberg eliminated all the snags in the Bugatti design, and, after the first few prototypes with Delage-type horizontal valves, a single overhead camshaft and inclined valves were

The Yankee Hispano – Wills Sainte Claire

adopted. Hydraulic four-wheel-brakes acting in 16 in. drums were standard, although in general, American manufacturers of the early 1920s were several years behind Europe in brake design, eschewing four wheel braking and clinging to that Edwardian relic, the band brake. However, the gargantuan V-12 Heine-Velox of 1921, as ugly as its name and at $17,000 America's costliest car, also had hydraulic f.w.b.

The Wills Sainte Claire was designed by the improbably-christened Childe Harold Wills, who had made his fortune in 1919 when Henry Ford had bought out all his associates in the Ford Motor Co: Wills' modest investment had become worth millions of dollars. It was a beautifully engineered car, utilising Wills' metallurgical expertise to the full. The engine was a 4-litre twin o.h.c. V-8 developing 65 b.h.p., with more than a hint of Hispano about it. Modestly priced at $2,475 in two-seater form, the Wills did not, however, survive 1927.

The Doble Steamer was built in Emeryville, near San Francisco, between 1924 and 1932 by its designer, Abner Doble, and his three brothers. Some 42 of these nobly proportioned machines were built, at prices ranging from $8,000 to $11,000. It was claimed that less than half-a-minute after throwing the switch to ignite the burner, enough steam would be generated to move the two-ton Doble and that the car could cruise at 60 m.p.h. and climb any hill where the tyres could grip.

133

For sheer size, no vintage American car could touch the Twin Valve Six McFarlan, built in Connersville, Indiana. Its six-cylinder T-head engine had a swept volume of 9·3-litres, 24 valves and 18 sparking plugs, and developed 120 b.h.p. But it was no match for the "volume classics" produced by Packard, Cadillac and Lincoln, and in August 1928, the McFarlan company was declared bankrupt.

Germany was in an unenviable state at the end of the war: the economy was crippled by galloping inflation, which made export to those few countries which could still buy "cars of ex-enemy origin" impossible; acute labour troubles affected most manufacturing industries, and the Allied blockade had left a dire shortage of raw materials, especially petrol, oil and rubber – in many cases, a set of tyres was worth more than the car they were fitted to. One would hardly think that there was a market here for high-powered luxury motors, yet Mercedes introduced a series of blown production 4- and 6-litre cars – when the throttle was hard down, a linkage engaged a clutch bringing the Roots-type supercharger into play; because it was not operating all the time, but only as a "desperation measure", it blew through the carburetter, rather than suck-

ing. This was not an entirely satisfactory arrangement, yet Mercedes persisted with it for many years.

In 1924 Mercedes and Benz entered into "an association of common interest": two years later they joined in official wedlock to form the Daimler-Benz AG, making "Mercedes-Benz" cars. The supercharged range continued to develop: in 1926 came the 6·25-litre "K", with a 90 m.p.h. maximum (which was by all accounts far in excess of the safe limit of the chassis); the following year came the "S", of 6·8-litres, capable of 103 m.p.h.; in 1929 "SS" and "SSK" (short chassis) models of 7·1-litres replaced the old model. Alongside them came the shatteringly fast two-seater SSKL and, at the end of the vintage period, the first of the celebrated 7·7-litre "Grosser" Mercedes, available with or without blower, appeared on the scene. At the other end of the capacity scale came the Henry-inspired twin o.h.c. Simson Supra S, an exceptionally well-designed 2-litre car in the Bugatti class.

1928 SSK Mercedes coupé

Motor Racing in the 1920s

After the war, serious motor racing did not get under way until 1919, when the Targo Florio and the Indianapolis 500 were held. The "Indy" was significant in seeing the new Duesenberg straight-8 engine in competition for the first time. Another famous straight-eight also made its first competitive appearance here, the Henry-designed Ballot, reputedly conceived on Christmas Eve 1918, and after a gestation period of 101 days, ready to race. Henry had achieved this miracle by doubling up on the $2\frac{1}{2}$-litre engine he had designed for the abortive Coupe de l'Auto of 1914, and installing it in a chassis of obvious Peugeot antecedents. Even so, the construction of a team of four cars inside three months was a remarkable feat, even if they weren't successful in the race, which was won by Wilcox' 1914 G.P. Peugeot. There was a moral victory for Henry in 1920 too, for the "500" that year was won by Gaston Chevrolet driving a Monroe with an engine based on the 1914 Peugeot. Second was René Thomas (Ballot) while Tommy Milton's Duesenberg came in third.

If the ghost of Ernest Henry walks anywhere, it is surely at Indianapolis, for his designs inspired a Wisconsin-born engineer, Harry Armenius Miller, to build racing engines.

Jimmy Murphy's 1921 Grand-
Prix winning Duesenberg

1919 Indianapolis Ballot

Jimmy Murphy installed one of these engines in a Duesenberg chassis and won the 1922 "500"; in 1923 an HCS-Miller came first. Then in 1924 and 1925 centrifugally blown Duesenbergs won: Miller went all out to develop a supercharger, and from then on Millers (now with only two valves per cylinder) were virtually invincible at Indianapolis. Between 1929 and 1965, Miller-type engines latterly known as Offenhausers won every Indianapolis 500 except 1939, 1940 and 1946.

The "Millercharger", running at five times crankshaft speed, could attain a speed of 37,450 r.p.m., at which its periphery was moving at 891 m.p.h. The finish on Miller's racing cars was legendary, and Bugatti bought a couple of Miller's revolutionary front-wheel-driven 1,500 c.c. racers in 1929 from racing drivers Léon Duray and copied the cylinder-head layout for his Type 50.

Miller really deserves far more recognition than he has previously been given: I would dearly love to see one of his 1927 10,154 c.c. V-16 marine racing engines in action – unblown, it developed 425 b.h.p. (the blower added another 50 per cent more power, it was stated). What a pity Miller only built one, unsuccessful, car round this power unit!

Apart from Millers, Indianapolis in the 1920s and early '30s was the happy hunting ground of the locally-built Model A Duesenbergs, but the greatest triumph of the Indianapolis Duesenbergs was Jimmy Murphy's easy victory in the 1921

137

The sheer size of Brooklands dwarfed the light cars competing in the 200-miles race, and diminished the effect of speed: "It was like flies crawling round the rim of a dinner plate"

French Grand Prix at Le Mans. Due partly to the effective hydraulic fourwheel brakes fitted to his car, Murphy came in 15 minutes ahead of the next man. This was the only time an American car ever won the French G.P. – in 1928 a lone Stutz came third.

While much of the racing at Brooklands during the 1920s followed the prewar pattern of handicapped races, a most important innovation was made in 1921, when the Junior Car Club held its 200-mile race for light cars of under 1,500 c.c. capacity. This was the first long distance race to be held for such cars, and attracted a fine entry, being won by H. O. D. Segrave driving a Coatalen-designed and Henry-inspired four-cylinder $1\frac{1}{2}$-litre Talbot-Darracq, which averaged almost 89 m.p.h., proof positive of the great strides in engine design made since pre-war days. Talbot-Darracqs (or their *alter ego*, Darracqs) also won in 1922 (driven by Kenelm Lee Guinness), 1924 (Guinness again) and 1925 (Segrave). In 1923, when the Talbot-Darracqs didn't run, Harvey's Alvis came in first, and in 1927 and '28, Malcolm Campbell won, driving a Bugatti on both occasions. By this time the race, which had been converted into a "road-racing" contest by the introduction of artificial corners on the track, had lost most of its spectator interest and it was not held again in its original form.

Instead, in 1929 the J.C.C. organised a "Double-Twelve" sports-car race based on the French 24-hour Le Mans contest but held in two 12-hour instalments, the cars being locked-up overnight. The race was narrowly won by Ramponi's Alfa Romeo from Davis' $4\frac{1}{2}$-litre Bentley, with a Salmson third.

Later in 1929, the British Racing Drivers Club organised a 500-mile race, which was notable for the first track appearance of Sir Henry Birkin's supercharged $4\frac{1}{2}$-litre Bentley, which retired, when a broken exhaust pipe set the body on fire, and a "normal" $4\frac{1}{2}$-litre Bentley, driven by Frank Clement and Jack Barclay came in first. In 1930 the Clerk of the Course, Lindsay Lloyd, who had served since 1908, retired, and was replaced by Percy Bradley, the instigator of the 200-mile event. New events and new cars were to radically alter the character of the track, and the pre-war racing cars which had formed such a colourful feature of the track during the decade were barred on the grounds of safety.

1923 supercharged Grand Prix Fiat

A diverting feature of British competitive motoring during the early 1920s was the hillclimbs held on public roads – quite illegally, but often with the connivance of the local constable. The best-known of these hills were Aston Clinton, South Harting and Kop, but an accident at the latter in 1925, when a Bugatti injured a spectator who was standing too near the track, was seized upon by the powers-that-be to put an end to competitions of this sort.

Henceforth hillclimbs had to be held on privately-owned courses, such as Shelsley Walsh, inaugurated in 1905.

In late 1921 a major change in Grand Prix racing came about when it was decided by the AIACR, the ruling body for motor sport, that the maximum capacity of 3-litres adopted after the Armistice for G.P. cars should be replaced by a 2-litre limit. The first French G.P. run under this new formula, held in 1922 in Alsace (recently recovered from Germany after 50 years' occupation), was dominated by the new six-cylinder Fiats from Italy's leading car-producing company which led for most of the way, while virtually every other car in the race save two Bugattis had retired or crashed by the halfway stage. Veteran driver Felice Nazzaro won by half-an-hour from the Bugattis, but his two team-mates, his nephew Biagio and

Pietro Bordino both crashed in the last ten laps, the former fatally. It was discovered that a flaw in the Fiat rear-axle casings had caused them to fracture near the hub, resulting in the loss of a wheel. A post-race examination found that the rear axle of the winning car was cracking, too . . .

The next year, Sunbeam's entries for the French G.P. were unashamed copies of the Fiats, which had won all the major contests in 1922: but Fiat had something far more interesting up their sleeve in the shape of a supercharged straight-eight. Unfortunately, the G.P. course at Tours was appallingly rough, and the Fiats digested a goodly quantity of flying grit, which did them no good at all, and Segrave on his Sunbeam went through to win.

Two months later, with the centrifugal superchargers that had let them down at Tours replaced by the more reliable Roots blower, the Fiats of Salamano and Nazzaro took the first two places in the Italian G.P. at the newly opened Monza autodrome: this was the first ever G.P. to be won by a supercharged car. Murphy's Miller was third; fourth and fifth came the astonishing Rumpler-designed Benz *Tropfenrennwagens* of Minoia and Horner, bullet-shaped rear-engined cars with swing-axle rear suspension, and more than a foretaste of the potent Auto-Unions of the late 1930s about them.

P2 Alfa-Romeo, 1924

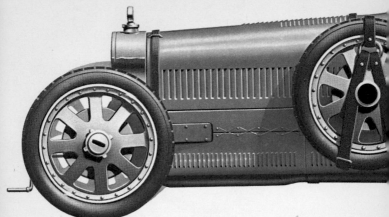

Alfa Romeo had built a team of blown sixes for the Italian G.P., but in practice their ace driver Ugo Sivocco crashed in one of these "P1s" and was killed, so the team was withdrawn in sympathy. In 1924 they introduced their P2 model, a supercharged straight-eight, the work of Vittorio Jano, lately employed by Fiat, which showed plainly in the design of the engine. These P2s won their first competitive outing at Cremona, then Campari won the French Grand Prix: the team crowned this by finishing 1-2-3-4 in the Italian G.P., ten laps ahead of the next man.

The P2s withdrew from the 1925 French G.P., held on the new Montlhéry race course, when Antonio Ascari skidded off the road in the wet and was fatally thrown from his Alfa. But the decisive victories of the Alfa Romeos in the Belgian G.P. at Spa and the Monza G.P. ensured their winning the newly instituted World Championship.

After this Jano devoted himself to developing the famous 1,500 and 1,750 c.c. six-cylinder sports cars.

The 1924 Grand Prix was a high point in motor racing in the 1920s. The 1925 Montlhéry event was poorly attended, and the drivers didn't care for the circuit, but it was a *succès fou* compared with the 1926 French G.P., which can have few rivals as the dullest motor race of all time. Run under a new 1½-litre formula, it was held on the isolated Miramas auto-

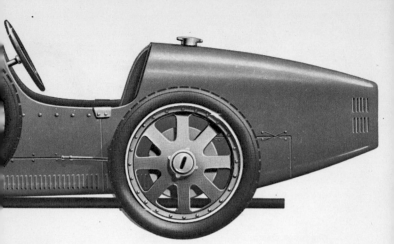

drome, situated in the Camargue. Hardly anyone bothered to enter, and the handful of spectators sweltering in the grandstand were treated to the thrilling spectacle of three Bugattis lined up for the start. One blew up before the halfway stage of the 100-lap race was reached, and the other two motored steadily round, the veteran Jules Goux coming in first at 68·16 m.p.h., 37 minutes ahead of the next (and last) man, Costatini.

These Bugattis were Type 39As, 1½-litre supercharged versions of the straight-8 Type 35 introduced in 1924, and one of the most famous racing cars of all time. You could buy one of these cars "over-the-counter" from the Bugatti works at Molsheim (Alsace), and during the late 1920s, when Grand Prix racing was at a very low ebb due to the piling of formula on formula, such Bugattis helped to keep the sport alive. Their claim of 2,000 race victories during the production span of the Type 35 (1924-31) was pretty meaningless, for this was due to sheer weight of numbers produced, and included many Bugatti-only events. One of the most handsome racing cars ever built, the Type 35 is more proof of Ettore Bugatti's ability as a sculptor (an ambition thwarted by the fact that his brother Rembrandt had already made his name in this field) than as an engineer; the engine, especially, worked far better than it theoretically had any right to. There is always room for

Straight-eight Delage, 1926

unconventionality in car design, but one feels that at times Bugatti was unconventional because he knew no better. He always insisted on the most scrupulously high standards from his workmen, and the factory was as neat and clean as an operating theatre. Had there been anything mediocre about the building of Bugattis, they probably wouldn't have worked at all. As it was, they were extremely potent.

One can draw many parallels between Ettore Bugatti and Parry Thomas – both produced cars which departed from conventional practice, both believed in symmetrical power units of almost architectural appearance, and both had the dream of producing the finest car the world had ever seen. Regrettably, Thomas was killed in 1927 right at the height of his powers, before he had the chance to develop fully his $1\frac{1}{2}$-litre "Flat-iron" Thomas-Specials, among the most advanced racing cars of the decade. Nothing about them was orthodox, although some of the details, such as the gearbox and rear suspension, had a hint of Bugatti. The eight steel cylinders were spigoted separately into the crankcase, and each pair of cylinders shared an hour-glass-shaped alloy water jacket. Turnbuckles pulled the head down on to the cylinders, and leaf valve springs were employed – a typical Thomas idiosyncrasy, which he shared with Frederick Lanchester.

Although the $1\frac{1}{2}$-litre formula was responsible for some disappointing races – another contribution to which was the proliferation of Grand Prix, which made preparing and racing a team of cars prohibitively expensive – some quite remarkable cars were produced under it.

Perhaps the greatest of these was the supercharged straight-eight Delage designed by Lory, which first appeared in 1926. The Delage team wasn't ready in time for the farcical French G.P. of that year, but in the Spanish G.P. and the British G.P. at Brooklands, 1½-litre Delages were second and first respectively, although the drivers suffered agonies from the proximity of the exhaust pipe to the pedals. For 1927, therefore, the exhaust was moved to the other side of the car. Other detail refinements were also carried out at the same time, and in their revised form these Delages — reputed to have cost £30,000 each to build – won all four Grands Prix (French, British, Italian and Spanish) in 1927. Despite the fiendish complexity of their twin o.h.c. engines, which had 23 spur gears driven from the nose of the crankshaft – eight for the camshafts, seven for the magneto, two each for the oil and water pumps and four for the supercharger – and 48 roller or ball bearings, the Delages were exceptionally reliable, and ten years later the young racing driver Richard Seaman was able to resurrect one of these cars and use it with great success in voiturette events against such potent machines as the most modern Maseratis and ERAs.

1926 Talbot-Darracq

Not so successful, perhaps, but of most advanced conception, were the 1926 straight-eight Talbots, the final racing cars from the Sunbeam-Talbot-Darracq group, whose financial status was sadly in decline. Designed by Bertiarone, these cars had supercharged twin o.h.c. engines set in a pressed-steel chassis consisting of parallel girders 10 in. apart, linked by vertical members. The body panels were screwed direct to this chassis, making an immensely rigid unit, and the axles passed between the upper and lower girders. The driver sat on the floor pan, with the propeller shaft from the offset engine running alongside him.

The waning fortunes of the S-T-D combine prevented these cars from ever really proving themselves, and in late 1927 all the Talbot racing cars were sold to Emilio Materassi, a wealthy Italian racing driver. During 1928 they enjoyed considerable success, but in September 1928 Materassi suffered a heart attack while competing in the Italian G.P., and his Talbot crashed into the crowd, with much loss of life. In 1929 the Materassi Talbots won some important victories, but the old P2 Alfas were resurrected, and faced with these and the new Maseratis, the Talbots quietly faded away.

Among the cars competing in the *formule libre* Spanish Grand Prix of 1926 was a truly remarkable 4-litre Sunbeam

Birkin's Brooklands Blower Bentley, 1930

driven by Segrave, which was to prove one of the most versatile racing cars of the 1920s. The engine was a supercharged V-12, composed of two 1924 2-litre six-cylinder G.P. blocks on a common crankcase, with roller bearings to crankshaft and connecting rods. In the Spanish event, the tubular front axle broke due to faulty boring when the car was lying second, but the car's subsequent career was varied, to say the least.

Segrave broke the land speed record with it later in 1926 at 152·31 m.p.h., and the Sunbeam, which acquired the name *Tiger,* competed in hillclimbs, sprints, and Continental road and track events before "settling down" at Brooklands, in company with a mate, *Tigress,* and two 2-litres – one known, appropriately, as the *Cub.* In the able hands of Kaye Don, *Tiger* broke the Brooklands lap record in 1929 at 134·2 m.p.h., and in 1930 raised this to 137·61 m.p.h.: it also won the fastest race at the track in the pre-1930 period, at 128·4 m.p.h.

Its great rival at Brooklands was the $4\frac{1}{2}$-litre single-seater supercharged Bentley of Sir Henry Birkin, which could lap fractionally faster. Bentleys, of course dominated the 24-hour "Grand Prix d'Endurance" sports car race at Le Mans, which they won in 1924, '27, '28, '29, and '30, but the sole entry of the marque in "real" Grand Prix racing was in the *formule libre* 1930 French G.P. at Pau, when Birkin came second in a "blower $4\frac{1}{2}$".

Birkin's addiction to supercharging seems to have been sadly misplaced, for the blown cars had nothing like the reliability of the standard Bentley product: their successes were hardly commensurate with the cost of the exercise.

147

Land Speed Record Cars

The 1920s saw a tremendous amount of activity in the record-breaking sphere, and during the decade the land-speed record passed for ever from the reach of the conventional type of motorcar. After Kenelm Lee Guinness had taken Hornsted's old record at Brooklands in 1922, Ernest Eldridge took his reconstructed FIAT *Mephistopheles* to Arpajon in France in 1924, where, driving a V-12 10½-litre Delage, the Frenchman René Thomas had just set up a new record of 143·3 m.p.h. After a certain amount of wangling to get past the regulation demanding a reverse gear, Eldridge broke Thomas' record by almost 2 m.p.h.

After that, the record fluctuated between the two Sunbeams, *Manitou* and *Tiger,* until in 1926 Parry Thomas entered the lists with his colossal ex-Zborowski V-12 *Babs* (née the *Higham Special*). He broke the record twice in 1926, at 169·3 and 171 m.p.h., but this was the last track car successfully to attempt the world's speed record, for Malcolm Campbell had constructed a vehicle with one aim in view – maximum speed in a straight line. Named *Blue Bird*, like most of Campbell's fast machines since 1911, the massive car had a 450 h.p. Napier Lion engine, similar to those used in the Schneider Trophy racing seaplanes, and achieved almost 175 m.p.h. Attempting to better this speed, Parry Thomas was killed on Pendine Sands in South Wales in early 1927.

Shortly afterwards Segrave travelled to Daytona Beach, Florida, with a gigantic brute of a car concocted by Louis

Segrave's 45-litre twin-engined Sunbeam

Coatalen from two V-12 Sunbeam *Matabele* aero-engines with a total capacity of 44,888 c.c. in a channel girder chassis with sidemembers two feet deep. The two engines, one front, one rear, were linked to a common gearbox driving the rear axle by side chains.

This awesome vehicle achieved 203·79 m.p.h. and Segrave was knighted for this feat. Not to be outdone, Campbell had now increased *Blue Bird's* power to 950 h.p., and in February 1928 he too went to Daytona and reached 207 m.p.h. – such cars were too big and powerful for the speed courses of the British Isles, as Jules Foresti had learned to his cost. He had constructed a beautiful straight-eight 400 h.p. car called *Djelmo,* in honour of its sponsor, the Egyptian Prince Djelal-ledin, which he had tried at Pendine. After the second crash, he gave up . . .

The Irving-Napier *Golden Arrow* reached 231 m.p.h. in 1929

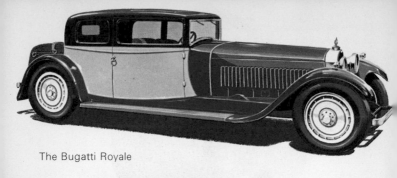

The Bugatti Royale

1935 Duesenberg J

Giants of the Depression

Shortly before the Depression, some of the most sumptuous cars of all time were introduced, in a curious parallel with the Mesozoic Period of geology when the mighty dinosaurs evolved to unparalleled size; and then vanished entirely in the face of an unforeseen cataclysm.

First among these saurians of the motor age, both in date of inception and in sheer bulk, came the Bugatti "Royale". As far back as 1913 Ettore Bugatti had considered producing a gigantic luxury car such as the world had never seen, but other preoccupations prevented him from realising his ambition until 1926. Based on a 1925 aero-engine design, the colossal eight-cylinder single o.h.c. engine of *La Royale* had a swept volume of 14·7-litres (reduced on production models to 12·8-litres) and an all-up weight of 770 lb., as much as a complete Austin 7. It developed 300 b.h.p. at 1,700 r.p.m. The car had a wheelbase of 14 ft. 2 in., and a three-speed gear in the back axle – low gear, for moving away from rest, direct drive, for normal motoring, and overdrive. In the latter ratio (2·66:1), the 2½-ton *Royale* was good for 120 m.p.h., with roadholding to match. Between 1927 and 1933 only six purchasers were willing to pay the 500,000 francs Bugatti demanded for a *Royale* chassis – so Bugatti adapted the *Royale* type engines for powering high-speed railcars: one reached a record 122 m.p.h. in 1936.

As arrogant in conception and execution as *La Royale,* but far more successful, was the Model J Duesenberg, which replaced the Model A in 1928. The Duesenberg company had been acquired in 1926 by Erret Lobban Cord, who always had an eye for the flamboyant (it was to be shown to the full in the 1937 front-wheel-drive Cord) and he instructed the Duesenberg brothers to build the finest and fastest luxury car in the world. The result was the model J, with a 6·9-litre twin o.h.c. straight-eight engine with four valves per cylinder and developing 265 b.h.p. at 4,250 r.p.m., mounted in a chassis of exceptional rigidity, available in two lengths, short (11 ft. 10 in. wheelbase) or long (12 ft. 9½ in.). Much use was made of aluminium, and of course the car had hydraulic fourwheel braking. Some 470 Model Js were built between 1928 and 1937, at prices ranging from $13,500 to $25,000 complete. In 1932 came the fabulous SJ, with a centrifugal blower running at five times crankshaft speed, raising the power to a claimed 320 b.h.p., and the top speed to 129 m.p.h. as against the J's maximum of 116 m.p.h.: the SJ could reach 100 m.p.h. from rest in 17 seconds. These Duesenbergs were quite untypical of the American motorcar of their period; they were certainly among the most elegant cars of the 1930s.

In 1930 Bentley Motors introduced a new 8-litre model, developed from their 6½-litre six-cylinder of 1925. This was

1930 8-litre Bentley

151

the most profitable car Bentley ever built, and exactly 100 were sold at prices up to £3,039 10s. complete.

Not, perhaps, quite a giant, but an impressive car by any standards, was the Lancia Dilambda. The Lancia company were already famous for their V-4 Lambda fast tourer, with its revolutionary combined chassis/body frame and sliding pillar ifs: now they intended to manufacture a luxury car, primarily designed for the American market. As bodies would be supplied by the best bespoke coachbuilders, such as Farina, the Dilambda had a more conventional chassis frame, still of immensely stiff construction, slung low to the ground by virtue of the independent front suspension. The Dilambda was powered by a 100 b.h.p. narrow-angle V-8 of just under 4-litres, capable of propelling the car's two-ton bulk at 80 m.p.h. Its success – some 1,700 were built in its five-year production life – was well-merited.

In 1929 Rolls-Royce introduced the Phantom II, much modernised, with an entirely new chassis, to replace the Phantom I: from 1930 it was available in tuned "Continental" form, and offered rapid, silent transport at speeds up to 90 m.p.h. allied to the greatest possible luxury.

Strictly outside the arbitrary "vintage" era but more than worthy of attention is a fascinating group of Vee-engined

Giant of the 1930s – the V-12 Hispano

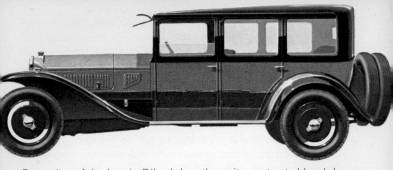

Progenitor of the Lancia Dilambda — the unit-constructed Lambda (1921-1930)

giants which appeared in the years 1930-32. King of these monsters was the 1931 V-12 9,424 c.c. Type 68 Hispano-Suiza, again based on Birkigt's wartime aero-engine experience, but with pushrods instead of the overhead camshaft: a couple of years later came the 68 *bis,* with an 11,300 c.c. engine developing 250 b.h.p.; speed was almost 110 m.p.h.

From Germany in late 1930 came the 7-litre Maybach which was soon supplanted by a similar 8-litre. The 7-litre had six speeds forward while the 8-litre had a five-speed gearbox (seven speeds after 1938) with a vacuum-assisted steering column change. So big it needed an omnibus licence, the 3-ton Maybach could move from 4 to 100 m.p.h. on top gear.

In 1932 Packard, Frankin and Pierce-Arrow, three of America's most respected luxury car builders, all introduced V-12s. The Packard, had a 7,292 c.c. engine: a prototype 6,145 c.c. Twin Six with front-wheel-drive was also built in 1932 but not proceeded with. A 1933 V-12 Packard Sport Sedan bodied by Dietrich won top honours in the Chicago Century of Progress Exposition of 1933, where Pierce-Arrow also caused a sensation with their streamlined V-12 Silver Arrow, with a $10,000 price tag.

Cadillac, too, introduced a V-12 but it was completely overshadowed by the mighty 7·3-litre V-16 of 1930, with pushrod o.h.v. actuated by hydraulic tappets. Not built for sheer speed, the Cadillac gave the ultimate in smooth and silent progress, in which to some extent it was rivalled by the 8-litre Marmon V-16 of 1931, of which around 470 were sold.

Pointers to the Future

Although these vast, lordly cars with their multiplicity of cylinders and fine coachwork were truly magnificent, in their heyday, you would have had to have stood for a very long time by the roadside before such a vehicle came by. But while you waited, dozens of cheap, boxy mass-produced family saloons would have whirred and chuntered by. For this was the first flowering of the motor age, when people of moderate incomes could afford to buy and run a motorcar.

Production had forged ahead in Britain, where the number of cars produced in 1929 (239,000) was more than twice the total of automobiles registered in 1914 - but in the latter year Ford had turned out 260,720 Model Ts in the U.S.A., half the country's total output. In 1929 the U.S. produced a fantastic 5,337,087 cars, a record unequalled for the next 20 years.

But there was a price to pay for this progress. The romance was fast going out of motoring, and driving in towns was already becoming a purgatory. The smaller car-building companies found themselves unable to cut their prices to compete with the major companies, but lacking the capital to

Straight-eight front-wheel-drive Alvis

expand sufficiently to go into mass-production. Some of the most respected names in motoring history disappeared from this cause between 1928-1932.

At first only a handful of enthusiasts bemoaned the passing of the high standards of workmanship and handling inherent in the cars of the 1920s, but it soon became all too obvious that designers had not entirely mastered the techniques of mass-producing durable, drivable cars.

The 1930 Burney Streamline was built by the designer of the R101 airship. It had a rear-mounted engine and all-round independent suspension. The type was later built under licence by Crossley.

BOOKS TO READ

The Complete Encyclopaedia of Motorcars Edited by G. N. Georgano. Ebury Press, 1968. Gives potted histories of over 4,000 makes of car, with nearly 2,000 illustrations. Invaluable for those interested in motoring history.

The Vintage Motor Car By Cecil Clutton and John Stanford. B. T. Batsford, 1961. An excellent guide to the leading vintage makes.

Power and Glory By William Court. Macdonald, 1966. A thorough and well-illustrated history of Grand Prix racing from 1906 to 1951.

The Longest Auto Race By George Schuster and Tom Mahoney. John Day, New York, 1966.

My Father Mr Mercedes By Guy Jellinek-Mercedes. Foulis, 1966.

Grand Prix Racing 1906-1914 By T. A. S. O. Mathieson. Connaisseur Automobile, Sweden, 1966.

German High-Performance Cars By Sloniger and Von Sersen. B. T. Batsford, 1965.

French Vintage Cars By John Bolster. B. T. Batsford and *Auto Sport*, 1964.

Annals of Mercede -Benz Motor Vehicles. Daimler-Benz, Stuttgart, 1961
From Engines to Autos By Frederick Schildburger. Daimler-Benz, Stuttgart, 1961.

The History of Brooklands Motor Course By William Boddy. Grenville, 1957.

The History and Progress of the Steam Engine By Elijah Galloway and Luke Hebert. London, 1832.

A Few Facts Concerning Elementary Locomotion Put Together by Francis Macerone. London, 1832.

A Narrative of Twelve Years Experiments 1824-1836 By Walter Hancock, Engineer. London 1838.

The following one make histories can be recommended:

Lanchester Motor Cars By Anthony Bird and Francis Hutton-Stott. Cassell, 1965.

Bugatti By H. G. Conway. Foulis, 1963.

The Bullnose Morris By L. P. Jarman and R. I. Barraclough. Macdonald, 1965.

The Chain-Drive Frazer Nash By David Thirlby. Macdonald, 1965.

The Vintage Alvis By Peter Hull and Norman Johnson. Macdonald, 1967.

Renault 1898-1966 By Yves Richard. Editions Pierre Tisné, Paris, 1966.

MUSEUMS TO VISIT

In Britain
Cheddar Motor Museum, Cheddar, Somerset
Glasgow Transport Museum, Glasgow
Herbert Art Gallery and Museum, Coventry
Hull Transport Museum, Hull, Yorkshire
Montagu Motor Museum, Beaulieu, Hampshire
Museum of Science and Industry, Birmingham 3
Science Museum, South Kensington, London S.W.7.
Shuttleworth Collection, Old Warden, Bedfordshire

In the U.S.A.
Harrah's Automobile Collection, Reno, Nevada
Long Island Motor Museum, Southampton L.I.

In Europe
Austria: Technisches Museum für Industrie und Gewerbe, Vienna 14
Belgium: Mahy Collection, Ghent
Czechoslovakia: Narodni Technike Museum, Prague 7
France: Conservatoire National des Arts et Métiers, Paris 3
    Musée d'Automobiles Anciennes, Clères, Nr. Rouen
    Musée de l'Automobile, Le Mans
    Musée Nationale de l'Automobile, Rochetaillée-sur-Saone, Rhône
    Musée Nationale de la Voiture, Compiègne, Oise
    Museon di Rodo, Uzes, Gard
    Renault Historical Collection, Paris
    The Museum, Autodrome de Linas-Montlhéry, Nr. Paris
Germany: Automobilmuseum der Daimler-Benz AG, Stuttgart-Unterturkheim
    Deutsches Museum von Meisterwerken, der Naturwissenschaft und Technik, Munich
Holland: National Museum van de Automobiel, Driebergen, Nr. Utrecht
Italy: Museo dell Automobile Carlo Biscaretti de Ruffia, Turin
    Museo Nazionale della Scienza e della Technica, Milan
    Padiglione Automobili d'Epoca, Monza
Norway: Norsk Teknisj Museum, Oslo
Portugal: Museo do Automovel, Caramulo, Nr. Coimbra
Spain: Réal Automovil Club de España, Madrid
Sweden: Skokloster Motor Museum, Lake Malaren, Nr. Stockholm
    Tekniske Museum, Stockholm, NO
Switzerland: Musee de l'Automobile, Chateau de Grandson, Lac de Neuchatel Verkehrshaus der Schweiz, Lucerne

INDEX

SOME OTHER TITLES IN THIS SERIES

Natural History

The Animal Kingdom
Animals of Australia & New Zealand
Animals of Southern Asia
Bird Behaviour

Birds of Prey
Evolution of Life
Fishes of the World
Fossil Man

Gardening

Chrysanthemums
Garden Flowers

Garden Shrubs

Popular Science

Astronomy
Atomic Energy
Computers at Work

The Earth
Electronics
Exploring the Planets

Arts

Architecture

Jewellery

General Information

Flags
Guns
Military Uniforms

Rockets and Missiles
Sailing
Sailing Ships & Sailing Craft

Domestic Animals & Pets

Budgerigars
Cats

Dog Care
Dogs

Domestic Science

Flower Arranging

History & Mythology

Discovery of
  Africa
  Australia
  Japan

Discovery of
  North America
  South America
  The American West